THE CAPTURE
OF
BILLY the KID

Edited by

James H. Earle

Creative Publishing Company
Box 9292, Phone 409-775-6047
College Station, Texas 77842

The Capture of Billy the Kid

The Capture of Billy the Kid.

(The Early West)
Bibliography: p. 149
Includes index.
1. Billy, the Kid. 2. Southwest, New—History—1848-
I. Earle, James H. II. Series: Early West series.
F786.B54C37 1988   364.1'552'0924   88-16227

ISBN 0-932702-44-9, 1500 copies

First Edition, First Printing

Copyrighted by Creative Publishing Company, 1988
The Early West, Phone 409-775-6047
Box 9292, College Station, Texas 77842

Dedication

Dedicated to

Bob McCubbin
Scholar of the Old West

The Capture of Billy the Kid

4

Table of Contents

5

INTRODUCTION

The Lincoln County historian, Maurice G. Fulton, gave a capsule account of Billy the Kid in a letter to me written in March 1953:

> In the Lincoln County War, there were higher-ups who pulled the strings, Billy the Kid and others being the puppets who carried the pistols and did the killings. The notorious Santa Fe ring was behind the Murphy-Dolan side; the McSween side had behind it Chisum and the larger percent of the Mexican population and almost the entire Anglo contingent in the Lincoln area. The Coes and Dick Brewer and others were good and "peaceable" men. Billy strayed into the region and aligned himself with that group which went by the name of *Regulators*. They were all mad about the killing of Tunstall and since Brady, the sheriff, was the tool of Murphy-Dolan, they took matters into their own hands. Billy was not the leader, but he was prominent and popular. He really emerged as the leader after the death of McSween. He lived at Fort Sumner a year and a half, adopting cattle stealing as a means of livelihood. He felt himself tricked by Gov. Wallace and John Chisum. His outbreak in the Carlyle killing brought down the

Introduction

wrath of the White Oaks people and resulted in Garrett taking the trail and finally capturing him at Stinking Springs. His trial and conviction followed. The escape from the old courthouse put him on a pedestal and made him famous, but doomed the Kid in the eyes of Gov. Wallace.

There was no one to save the Kid . . . he was out of favor with Chisum and Catron, the two "mighty opposites" at the top. Garrett had the approval of both groups. The killing at Fort Sumner followed. I doubt if Garrett would have killed the Kid had he not been surprised by the Kid's appearance that night at Maxwell's.

Colonel Fulton dug into Lincoln County history and the life of Billy the Kid for over thirty years while a number of participants were still alive, and his views deserve respect. He placed great value in his interviews with survivors of the period, feeling that although they might not be entirely accurate, they provided insight and understanding of the people and the time.

Cal Polk's account of the pursuit and capture of Billy the Kid was not known to Colonel Fulton, but it provides the kind of insight he valued so highly. The current reigning authority on Lincoln County, Nora Henn of Lincoln, New Mexico, mentioned to me in the summer of 1987 that she had heard that a manuscript written by Cal Polk was in

The Capture of Billy the Kid

the possession of the Panhandle Plains Museum. I immediately took off for Canyon, Texas, where the staff at the museum quickly and graciously found the Polk manuscript and allowed me to copy it.

Polk's uninhibited and crudely written account of a wild seventeen year old cowboy out on a lark was of such interest to me I sent a copy to Jim Earle, whom I knew would share my enthusiasm for it. This little book is the result.

It is rare that something new and original relative to Billy the Kid surfaces. The ground has been covered for many years by scores of diligent researchers of varying competence. The accounts of Cal Polk, Louis Bousman, Charles Siringo, Jim East, and Pat Garrett, plus the Charley Foors map have been merged together to give primary information on the capture of the Kid. Contemporary newspaper reports conclude the book.

This book merits publication because it is new source material by actual participants and because it "tells it like it really was;" above all, it makes fascinating reading.

Robert G. McCubbin
El Paso, Texas
April, 1988

Introduction to
Cal Polk Version

As a young Texas cowboy, Cal Polk rode with Pat Garrett in the posse that captured Billy the Kid. He is the only person in the posse who made a written eyewitness account of it.

Cal Polk was born in Caldwell County, Texas, and married Anne Hampton who also was from the Prairie Lea community. They moved to Holdenville, Oklahoma, in the Creek Indian Nation. In 1896, he wrote an account of his life covering his experiences as a cowboy. In 1901, he added 24 pages to the 93 pages already recorded. This manuscript was written in a legal size ledger book. About twenty years ago, I was privileged to read it and at that time, I made a xerox copy. My wife is a granddaughter. In 1938, Jessie Polk and I were married. Since 1970, we have covered the areas which he traveled as a cowboy and are impressed by the accuracy of his narrative.

We gave a copy of our copy to the Panhandle Plains Museum at Canyon, Texas, because they have Cal Polk's name on file as a LX Ranch cowboy. We recently visited Luling, Prairie Lea, and Lockhart because of our family interest. Mrs. Esther Deviney at Martindale, extended the hospitality of her home and mentioned the Caldwell County Historical Commission during our visit. We told her that a copy of our copy of the Cal Polk manuscript would be prepared and mailed to her to present to that commission because Cal was a native of Caldwell County,

The Capture of Billy the Kid

and that is where his story began. We are informing the Panhandle Plains Museum so its management will know that this copy has been made available to Cal Polk's home community.

By the age of seventeen, Cal Polk had made two cattle drives to Dodge City and become a top ranch hand at the LX and helped in the capture of Billy the Kid. He was a protege of Jim East, who camped with him on the range and taught him to read and write. Cal's ability to remember names and places was outstanding. Without background material and guideline information, the manuscript is of little if any value. It is difficult to read and the spelling is almost funny.

Cal Polk died in 1904 and his widow lived until 1944. When she died, one of the three daughters took possession of the ledger book and manuscript. When she died, her son took charge of it and our copy was made from the original and it was returned to that grandson. Today, he claims that he does not know where it is. Without proper care, it may have disintegrated. If it is found, my wife and her cousins have committed it to the Panhandle Plains Museum.

There are many reference points given in the composition of the Cal Polk story. After leaving Caldwell County, points of interest in part are as follows; Fort Worth, Saint Jo, Red River Crossing, Indian Nation, Wichita Mountains, Dodge City, Southeast Colorado, No Mans Land, Texas Panhandle, the LX Ranch, Tascosa, Rabbit Ear Mountains, Anton Chico, Fort Sumner and White Oaks.

Cal tells the story about the party of seven men on a survey crew in the White Oaks area. The cowboys met them one day and picked up their destroyed bodies shortly thereafter. The cowboys took time to give them a burial. Now this may be the only record on earth of those seven men being killed. It is possible that there are relatives today who tell the story that their grandfather and great uncles were lost with a survey crew in New Mexico in the 1880s.

He also relates the story of the cattle drive where Cal worked for Trail Boss M. A. Withers. Oklahoma State University at Stillwater has a book with the title, *Trail Drivers of Texas*. That is my school and I have read the book. Cal Polk's report is identical to that book as relates to people and important facts about the drive.

During the first reading of this material, I assumed that Cal Polk worked for the Bar X Ranch but my research resulted in a complete misfit of facts. My thoughts on the matter suggested that his ranch identification might be the branding iron so I made the figure with ink and put it to a blotter and there was the LX. Everything fell into place at that point.

At Holdenville, Hughes County, Oklahoma, Cal Polk served as U. S. Deputy Marshal and later as City Marshal. The office of sheriff at Holdenville has a plaque on display with the names of *Officers of The Law who Gave Their Lives in The Line of Duty*. The name of Cal Polk is listed there. He died from a wound inflicted accidently by his own gun. His widow and their five children moved to a farm. The three girls and two boys are deceased but have surviving children, and grandchildren.

Edgar L. McVicker
Burneyville, Oklahoma
January 1988

11

The Capture of Billy the Kid

Cal Polk (right) when he was city marshal of Holdenville,
Oklahoma. (Courtesy of Panhandle Plains Museum)

Cal Polk

CAL POLK VERSION

The following version of the pursuit and capture of Billy the Kid and his gang at Stinking Springs is given as Cal Polk wrote it. This material has been taken from Cal Polk's autobiography that is dated January 25, 1896. A copy of it is in the Panhandle-Plains Historical Museum in Canyon, Texas, donated to them by Edgar and Jessie McVicker, descendents of Cal Polk.

The first paragraph is the beginning of his life story. The remainder of his account is limited to his participation in the tracking and arrest of the Kid, and his experiences in New Mexico shortly afterwards.

The misspelled words and incorrect grammar have not been changed. Cal Polk's story is given below as he wrote it.

The Editor

13

The Capture of Billy the Kid

LIFE OF C. W. POLK
Commenced January 25, 1896

I was borned in Caldwell Co Tx near Prairie Lea on Jan 8th 1863 and when about 6 years old my hold delight was to learn how to ride and rope and be a cow boy. I soon learnt how to ride a stick horse and rope the milk calvs in the lot. one of my cousins was living with us. By the name of Lum Woods. I was about the same sized & we was in kind of devilment. One day Lumm & I saw a bunch of cattle come up to where the salt longs were at to lik the salt. We opend the lot gate and got around them & run them in the lot. They was a (?) yearling in the bunch & I had saw cow boys rope cattle with the end of the rope tide around the horn of the saddle. So I thought I would be like a cow boy and I tide one end around my wast and roped the yearling with the other end. The wild anamal run to the gate and broke it down & tore out across the prairrie pitching and baling while I was squaling for ma to come quick. I was Ridind flat on the grun all the time.

. . . .

BEGIN THE BILLY THE KID PART

They was a heep of cattle stealing goin on at that time and they was several ranches up and down the Canadian River hired a man by the name of Frank Stuart to

14

stay in New Mexico and watch to find out if inney of the
Panhandle cattle was stolen & carried that way. In the winter Moor received a letter from Stuart telling him that Billy
the Kid and his men was a going toworge the White Oaks
with five hundred head of stolen cattle from the Panhandle
so Moor started five of us down there to see about it. He
put Jim McClarrity boss of the crowd.

After traveling a few days we caught up with Billy.
He had a hurd and 23 white men and a niggro with him.
They was in camp for dinner when we rode up. Billy asked us down and take dinner with him. We got down and
eate dinner, then Jim told him we wanted to look thru his
hurd. He said all rite, and told some of his hands to go
and round them up. We all mounted our horses and started
toworge the hurd. I nodist that Billy kept his winchester
in his hand and when we got to the hurd, Billy said there
they are, go in and look at them. As soon as we got in the
hurd we saw they all belonged to the LX and LIT Ranches.
Jim Rode back to Billy and said old boy these are our
cattle.

He wheeled his horse a round and said, there they are.
you can take themm, but you will take a heap of hot led
before you do. Of corse we did not want any cattle then.
We turned and rode easy, and I did not try to keep from

The Capture of Billy the Kid

riding in the lead for about 5 miles. We returned to the Ranch and told all about it.

The cattlemen up and down the river all raised cane and said they was goin to send 150 men after them desperados and the cattle. The Ranch men sent down to Austin, Texas and got papers to go into New Mexico after Billy the Kid and his out fit. Me and Jim East started south with Charley Cirringos out fit. after we had traveled three days Moor sent a man to over take us and bring the out fit back. He wanted to send us after Billy the Kid. They evening we got to the Ranch. While crossing the river on ice just after dark our chuck wagon broke thrue. We managed to get our horses out and went on to the Ranch, half froze which was a bout one half mile from the river.

The next morning we all went back to get the wagon out. We first build up a big fire on the bank and then draught straws to see who had to go in and cut it out. Me and Charley Cirringo was the unlucky boys.

We commence cutting a road from the edge of the water thrue the ice. We would cut out a block then sink it down and shove it under the ice on one side to get it out of the road. We kept on this way until we got to the waggon. then got the ice cut loose all around it. I tide a rope to the tong and carried the end to the boys on at the bank to help us pull. They pulled on the rope while me and

Charles A. Siringo (left) and W. O. Sayles as Pinkerton detectives in about 1893.

Charley got behind and pushed it. This way we got it out. When we got to the fire we looked as blue as indego. But it never hurt us. We stayed at the Ranch until next morning getting ready to start after the Kid.

When we got ready to go Moor did not have but five men that would go out of 25. these was C.W. Polk, James East, Lon Chambers, Lee Smith and Charly Cirringo, he was the Boss. and a cook, cuck wagon with 4 good mules. Each one of us carried one good horse a peace. While

17

The Capture of Billy the Kid

Charley carried too, and we had to hall corn to feed them on. We started on the 22nd day of Nov 1880 and went up to the LIT Ranch above Tascosa that night. The LIT outfit sent a wagon, cook and five men named as follows Louis Bosman, Monroe Harris, Tom Emray, Billy McKoley, and Bob Roberson for a Boss. While the LS Ranch sent three boys by the name of Bob Williams, Uncle Jimmie and Big Foot Wallace. The Panhandle cattle men could not get 150 men to go. The boys would quit there jobs in the dead of winter before they would go out. Out of 300 men they was only 13 that would go.

We started out to the LX Ranch that night. The snow was from 6 inches to 12 inches deep. The next night we got to Troheo (?), a small Mexacan town. There a man by the name of Johonson sent a wagon and a cook. So we had 3 wagons, 3 cooks, and 13 boys. We started on the next night. We got to a little Mexacan town and there they give us a big farwell dance for a send off.

The next morning Charley started on ahead to Las Vegas on a buck board with the male carrier to get corn. He told us to go to Antion Cheeko on the Pacos River, and there wait untill he came with the corn. We went ahead and got there on Sunday at 12 oclock. Just as we all rode up into town the cathlick church broke and the Mexacans coming out of it. They all stoped and gazed at us, and

18

wonderd what was the matter. We all had 2 belts full of cartidges a peace around us and was armed to the teeth with six shooters Bowie knives and Winchesters on our saddles.

Bob went and got a Doby Wall waggon yard to camp in while we was there from a merchent by the name of Stap Nelson. He was married to a Mexacan woman. The next day we all taken in the town sights and that night we all got big bells, tin cans, hornes and every thing we could find to make a nois with and shivered the town. We would march up the streets beating and ringing. You could not hear anything. When we would get to a saloon, we would go in it the same way. The bartender would stand back and laugh until we stope the noise. The we would tell him to setum up. He would set out a gallon of muscal. We would drink all we wanted and then strike out for another one the same way. It wasn't long until we did not have a man that was able to ring a bell or beat a can. But we findly made it back to camp and sleep all the next day.

We got up just before night and the Mexacans come and told us they was agoin to give a big dance for our spechel bennefit and of corse this suited us. We all went and had a good time until 12 oclock when Bob Roberson and Jim East went in town and got a big tin bucket full of miler class whiskey and another one full of muscal then come

The Capture of Billy the Kid

back and went to passing it a round with tin cups to drink out of. The girls and all pertook of it and in ten minutes they was not a Mexacan in the house could stand on ther feet and if one would get up and try to stand we would give it a nother dost.

The next day we all rested again in our little beds and getting ready to bum around at night they was. All way a few Mexacans that would follow us a round in order to get drinks. So that night Bob Roberson went to a drug store and got 25 cents worth of croton oil and went to a saloon and there we bought a quart of muscal then put the oil in it and give it to our Mexacan bums and that was the last time we saw them.

The next day we all went broke on a horse race. We run a broke down cow pony against a dead fast race horse for all the monnie we had and 5 gallons of muscal. We run rite in the streets of Antion Chicko. I rode our horse while a small mexican rode the other. We run 400 yards. Our boys was standing on the side of the track about 50 yards from the out come. When me and mexacan went down to start, I got a big run on him and went off a head but about one hundred yards he overtakes me and went on. And when he got to the crowd his horse dashed out and stoped. I then pased as he was getting started again. But he pased me before I could get thrue the poles. His horse was fast

enuff to give mine half way thru and then pased him before he got out.

We has all dead broke but they was 400 pounds of
parched coffee in the wagons. Belong to the Bar X and LIT
out fits and we made it take place of monnie. You could
see a boy go and fill up both over coats pockets full of coffee and strike out trading every day.

Charley never got there for 10 days and when he
come, we just had a nuff coffee for breakfast. We would
attend a dance every other night. While we was camped
there one of our boys by the name of Billy McColey shot a
Mexacan. The way it come up, old Stape Nelson owned
the yard we was camped in and had a fuss with the Mexacans in a settlement between them. The Mexacans went a-
cross the street. About that time Billy come along with a
quart of Red licker in him. Nelson told Billy about it. Billy
said less go and get him and make him settle. They went
and got him and when about half way across the street the
Mexacan stoped and said he would not go any farther.
Billy reached for his 45. The Mexacan grabed him. They
both turned around like a windmill and the pistol fired.
The Mexacan run one way and Billy the other.

He come rite to camp half scared to death and told
Bob Roberson he had killed a Mexacan. The coral we was
camped in was a doby wall fence about 8 feet high and

The Capture of Billy the Kid

one area in it with only one gate. In 10 minutes they was 6 Mexacans officers come to the gate and wanted Billy. Bob told them they can't not get him. We was all setting a-round camp rubing up our guns to no they was all rite. As we exspected to haft to use them soon. The officers went back and you could see Mexacans agoing from one door to another with all kinds of old rusty guns and in 2 ours they had all got in a bunker and sent a boy with a note riten in inglish telling us they must have that man killer. Bob rote on the back of the note you cant get him. But you can get a fite as all my boys is eaching for it to come off.

We heard nothing more and that night we went on gard. The next morning just as the big green sun was com-ming up, we heard the sound of a war bugle. The Mexacans had went and got a compeney of troops and sorounded the town. In five minutes up comes a boy with a note from the captian. It read this way. We have got the town sorounded and you must give up Billy McColly in 20 minutes or I will make a charge on you. Bob set down and answered it. He says you can pitch and charge, but you cant get him as long as one of us has got a button left on our coats.

In about 20 minutes a nother note came. Saying we will give you a nother chance and then we will set the town on fire if you dont give him up. Bob scribled this won on the back of it, you can burn the town if you want

22

to for we can hitch up our 3 wagons and pull them out of town. And if you croud us, they will be some thing left to put in a nuse paper at this time. Jim East got a horn and began to blow it while I climed up on on the doby wall and began to shake a red under shirt at the Mexican troops.

By this time things began to look sqwaly. The shot Mexacan was not dead but badly wounded. Old Nelson who was the cause of the shooting was scard and afraid if we left the Mexacans would eate him up blood raw without salt. He struck out to try and make peace. Before we left he went to the wounded man and a greed to pay the doctor bill and all expences and give him 200 dollars in cash and this was excepted and he settled the hole thing that way. Then the troops come up to see the out fit they was agoing to contend with one our before that, the captan told Bob he was a fraid if he charged on us he would get his men all killed by them Texas cow boys.

While we was there Billy the Kid come in town one night and stole 3 good horses from Mexacans. He then rote a letter to Frank Stuart telling us to not come no further, that he did not want to fite us. But if we came to come a shootin. This was strate goods but we had it to face. As you will see later we had all went deeply in debt while we was there and exspected Charley to come with a pocket

23

The Capture of Billy the Kid

full of monnie from Las Vagas. But when he come we was broke. He got to gambling up there and lost all the monnie the LX firm started him with and he had to give a check on them for the corn, so we had to give checks here they same way.

We rigged up and started for the White Oaks and when we got to the Rosewel Wells there we met Barney Mason a ex chum of Billy the Kid. But now a deputy sheriff of Lancorn Co. under Pat Garrett. He told us that all of Billys men had quit him except 6, and a croud of 80 men from the White Oaks had them rounded up in Jim Gratehouse is ranch and was waiting for us to get there and help make the fite. But of corse we was in no hurry and when we got there, Billy had come out and killed the leader Jim Carlile and gone.

Then the sheriff of Lancon County taken charge of us. All except a nuff of the men to take the wagons on to the White Oaks. So Pat started with us south east to old Ft. Sumner.

We got there just before night. We stoped and put our horses in a old soldier hospittle that had been deserted and we camped in a little house clos to it that night. We was all in the room playing poker, but Lon Chambers he was on gard out side. The snow was about 12 inches deep and the

24

Cal Polk

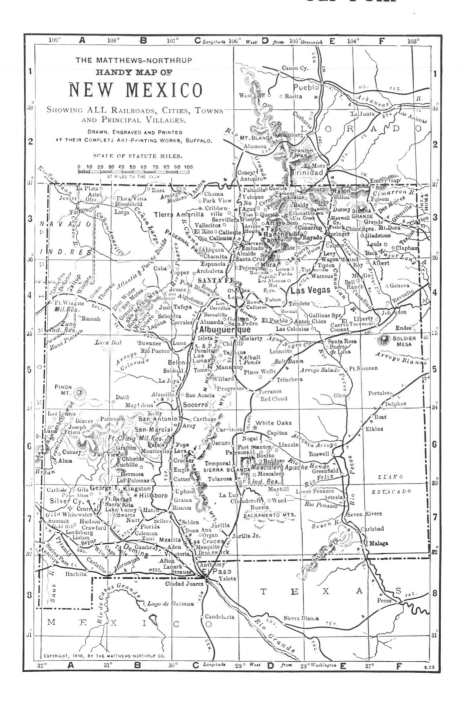

THE MATTHEWS-NORTHRUP

HANDY MAP OF

NEW MEXICO

SHOWING ALL RAILROADS, CITIES, TOWNS
AND PRINCIPAL VILLAGES.

DRAWN, ENGRAVED AND PRINTED
AT THEIR COMPLETE ART-PRINTING WORKS, BUFFALO.

SCALE OF STATUTE MILES.

0 10 20 30 40 50 60 70 80 90 100

67 MILES TO THE INCH

COPYRIGHT, 1898, BY THE MATTHEWS-NORTHRUP CO.

The Capture of Billy the Kid

moon was shining bright on it that made it light so you could see a man 300 yards off.

All at once Lon come to the door and said see some well armed men comming. We grabed up our guns and stept out in the shade of a high doby wall. They come on up until about 10 yards of us. When Pat Garrett spoke and said throw up your hands, at that moment they jerked gons out and they big shooting came off. They was about 40 shots fired. When the smoke got out of my face so I could see I saw one mans horse running in a circle and come back to us. When he got clos he said don't shoot any more for I am killed. We went to him. His name was Tom Ofalyar. We taken him off his horse. He was shoot thrue the breast and only lived about ten minutes and died.

Garrett then ordered us to get on our horses and follow the trail in the snow which we could see for 50 yards a head. You see Billy had lots of Mexacans friends that was carrying him nuse all the time so he new where we was and where our horses was and he thought he would come and steal our horses and then whip us. But he sliped up on that.

After we had gone on his trail a short distance we nodist blood a long on the snow from a wounded horse of thairs. We rode on ther trail untill about 2 oclock in the morning. When we come in sight of there horses tide in

Cal Polk

Tom O'Folliard, the Kid's closest friend and constant companion.

front of a little house that had been a ranch, but was vacant. We got down tide our horses and left too men with them. The ballance of us sliped up to a little spring branch which run along in front about 20 steps from the door. There they all stoped except mc and Jim East. We crauld up and went all around the little house to see if they was any port holes in it.

The house was sollid made of rock and no holes in it. Only one door, and no shuter to it. They horses was tide to a pole that stuck out over the door. We could here them snooring in side the wall which was about 4 feet from me and Jim. We then went back to the craud at the branch

The Capture of Billy the Kid

and told them how every thing was shaped up. We put some blankets down on the snow under the bow of the hill and lay down on them. We could lay there until day light half froze. Just at sun up we heard them talkin and getting up and in a few minutes a man come out with a morat in his hand to feed his horse. His name was Charley Bodder. Just as he was putting the morat on his horse we all raised up on our kneese and drewe a beed on him with our winchester. He looked over his sholder and saw us. Pat told him to throw up his hands.

He said all right in the minnet as he taken his hands down from the horses head, he jerked out 2 pistols and fired at us and at the same time we fired. They was three shots hit him one in the leg and too in the body. He droped his pistols and come realing toworge us. He said some thing like I wish, I wish, and then said blood is cloging in my mouth and fell acrost one of our boys, Lee Smith. He roled him over to one side and there he froze in a short time and lay there all day. In a few minets after the shooting, Billy cride out is that you Pat out there. Pat says yes, then Billy says Pat why dont you come up like a man and give us a fair fite. Pat said I dont aim to. Billy says that is what I thought of you, you old long legged S. . .B. and then every thing hushed for a while.

All at once some of the boys nodist that they was

28

Henry McCarty, alias Billy the Kid, is shown here in his most famous photograph that was made in about 1880.

The Capture of Billy the Kid

reaching out at the door and cutting the horses loose and leading them in the house. They had got 2 in, and just as they got a nother one in the door, we fired on him and droped the horse dead in the door. We then shot the ropes in to the others was tide with and turned them loose. Billy and his men was afraid to get in front of the door to pull the dead horse out of the way, and this blocked every thing. They aimed to get the horses in and mount them and come out a fiting for their lives. But they couldnt get over the dead horse in the door.

They was 2 boys went up on a little hill and comence shooting at the house. The horses in side got scard and was a bout to run over Billy and his men, so they turned them loose and out they come over the dead horse. As quick as they got out from the house we rounded them up and caught them. Pat sent a man to Willcoxes ranch after some grub which was about 6 or 8 miles while we build up a big fire to warm by. While we was warming, Billy said Pat have you got any thing out there to eate. Pat said yes. Billy said we have got some in here if you will let us come and get wood to cook it with. Pat says all rite you all can come out after wood if you want too. Billy says you go to H. . . you cowardly S. . .B. and then he hushed.

He would crack jokes where we could here them all day as if nothing was the mater. we garded there all day and built up a big fire up the branch about 200 yards and all got warm and cooked supper and while we was eating just at sundown, we saw a little white rag stuck out at the winder on a stick shaking. And in a few minets Mr. Ruderbay come out with his hands up. He then come on up to us where we was eating supper and told Pat that Billy wanted to surrender under sun up and wanted to know where Pat would carry them. Pat says to Las Vagas. Ruderbay said if we hafto go to Las Vagas, we will die rite here for the Mexacans will mob us there. Pat says we will carry you to Santafee.

Ruderbay says if you will see us safe to Santefee jale we will surender. This was agree on. So the boys come on out and left the arms in the house. When they got to us they all shuck hands with every man then set down and supper. And after supper we all mounted our horses. I took Billy the Kid up behind me while the other boys doubled up on ther horses and we started to Willcoxes ranch a bout 6 miles. Billy made me a present of his Winchester and Frank Stuart took his fine Bay mair. We got to the ranch at 9 oclock and stade untill morning then got a wagon and put the prisners in it while the other boys rode horse back.

We had to go to Las Vagas to get a train for Santefee. We traveled day and night to beet the mob back so the

The Capture of Billy the Kid

nuse would not get there first. We got to Las Vagas one evening and had to gard the jale that night to keep the Mexacans from takin the prisners out and hanging them

The next morning we taken the prisners out and put new chains on them and carried them in the car and chained them to the seats. The train men was making up there train to start to Santafee.

Me and Jim East thought that we would stay in Las Vagas and have a good time, while the rest of the boys went to Santafee. So we bid them all good bye and left them waiting for the train to get ready to start. Me and Jim started down in town and went into a saloon. While we was in there a Mexacan come in drunk and said in spanish to the bar tender the Mexacans is agoin to kill them prisners up at the train. I told Jim what he said and we finished up and started toworge the depot and when we got in sight of it, I saw there was about 300 Mexacans with all kinds of rusty goons a round the cars and 2 of them had ther guns Drawed on the Engineer and would not let him move.

We broke across the street to the hotel and got our guns and when we got to the craud we helt our guns down by our legs and worked our way thrue the crowd as if we was pasengers and when we jumped on the steps we then turned and threw down on the Mexacans. I looked and saw

32

Cal Polk

A drawing of Sheriff Pat F. Garrett that appeared in his book, THE AUTHENTIC LIFE OF BILLY THE KID.

Pat Garrett standin in the car door with his 45 in his hand. He said come in side boys and get at a winder. We went in just at that time, Frank Stuart who was at the other door cried out, gentlemen they is agoin to be a fite here and all that wont take a hand in it had better get out.

Of corse the drumers and others got ther grips and never taken time to tell us goobye. But they was 2 old long hungry looking men from up about Denver said they had not killed a Mexacan for 2 weeks and was Blood thurstay and would go in the fight for Pass time. They went down under ther seats and draught out some old long Buffalo guns and got at a winder. The mob ho wanted to linch Billys crowd was increasin all the time and was led By the

33

The Capture of Billy the Kid

Sheriff ho was a mexacan. Pat Garrett Says Boys Dont Burn Powder for nothing. When the first shot is fired all of you Kill a man Every shot and we will unchane the Prisners and arm them.

We was all at the winder on our Kneese with our guns stuck out at it while Pat was at one Door and Frank Sturt at the other. I had a Bead Draw on a Big Fat Greezer. They helt us ther in this shape for one our. And all at once a Depety United States Marchel jumped up on they ingin with his 45 in his Right hand and he Run and grabed the leaver with his left hand and pulled it wide open. The ingin spun on the track for about 5 minutes then it run out from among the greezers.

So me and Jim went on to Santefee with the Boys. We got thrue and landed them in Jale and started Back the next morning. We got to Las Vagas and stade 2 days and then started to the White Oaks one hundred and 50 miles where our wagons was at. The snow was very Deep and it was a hard trip to make, But after 5 Days hard travel we reached the White Oaks on our Broke Down horses.

Frank Sturt and Pat Garrett staid in Las Vasgas and in a few Days we saw in a paper that mr Sturt and Garrett had got $1800 Reword for Ketching the Kids Band. So when Mr Sturt come Down to the White Oaks and we wanted our Part of the Reward he Denide getting it for a

34

while. But when we put a Rope Round his neck and led him out to a Big Pine tree and threw the Rope over a Big limb and told him to say his Prairs as this was his last chance to say them, he looked up at the limb and said Boys I did get that monnie and I will whack up with you all, Rather than to Die. And this he Did and left the out fit.

We then had monnie to spree on for a while we staid there in camps for a Bout one month and it snowed very near every Day. While we was ther they had a Election for officers in the town so we all met one night and every man rote out his ticket and Droped it in a hat. They was about 50 men there and when they all voted, they was over 300 votes to count. This town was composed of tough men such as gamblers, saloons, and desperados. It was a comon thing to see a man shot Down there on the streets. They was killed there one Day while we was there. We fiendly moved out one mile from town so we could Kill a beef and not have so many neighbors to devide with.

We heard that a man By the name of Pat Coglon had charge of the cattle that Billy had stolen from our Ranch. Billy would steal them and Coglon would sell them. So me and Charley Ciringo went Down to see Mr Coglon. When we got there we found 3 head of our cattle in his Butcher Pen. He was Runing a Beef market. We told him not to kill

The Capture of Billy the Kid

Colonel and Mrs. Maurice G. Fulton were photographed at the site of the rock house at Stinking Springs where the Kid was captured.

them nor for him not to kill any more of the Bar X cattle. He had a Blood thursty craud of greezers around him and he told us a near way to go Back thrue some mountains to the White Oaks. So as our horses was teard and it was late we tride the near cut and when we got about 2 miles we come to a deep canyon and a trail to go Down in it. Brush was thick on Both sides of the trail.

Charley was a head Riding a mule and when we about half way Down the hill Bang Bang went guns on Both sides of the trail. Charleys mule fell and my horse whirled a round I saw a man Runing thrue the Brush. I Drew my

A close-up photograph of the foundation of the rock house at Stinking Springs. The Fultons were photographed here in about 1925.

winchester and fired 3 shots at him. But he was soon out of sight in the Brush. I turned then and cald Charley and told him them Damn Cowards was gone. Charley come up and we examend our horses. I found that Charleys mule was shot in the top of the sholders But was able to travel. My saddle had 2 Bulets holes in it and a Pair of Blankets that was tide on Behind the saddle had a hole Plowed thrue them By a Ball.

We mounted and got to camp about Eleven oclock that night on our Broke Down anamals and had menny tails to tell the Boys about our trip. The next morning we

The Capture of Billy the Kid

moved our camp about 12 miles out in the mountains So we could hund game as they was lots of it there of all Kinds. We was waiting for spring to come and the snow to melt so we could Round up Pat Coglons Rance and get our cattle.

While we was camped there one eavening about 4 oclock a out fit of Survayors come By our camp in a hack and 4 horses and 7 men. They stoped and got watter at our camp. They was on they way to the Snowey mountains to Do some survaying for the State. They traveled on about 2 miles that night. We turned our horses loose all But one we cept up to get them up on of a morning. The next morning its was Big foots time to get them up. He started and was gone about one our when we seen him comming in a full Run with his hat in hand crying out indians indians. I found a mans head cut off lying in the Snow.

We then made a Rush for our guns and all started loaded down with catridges. When we got to where Big foot had found the head there was a trail of between 3 and 4 hundred horses had went a long. We went a short Distants back on the trail. There we found a mans Body and a Bout one hundred yards forther we found the hack and other six men in every direction from it all Butchered up.

It seems that every man was Runing when Killed. The

38

A rock house of the type that the Kid and his gang were trapped in at Stinking Springs on December 23, 1880.

horses and every thing was gone But the Hack. This was Done By old Geronimos Band as we found out later. We Dug a long grave with a spade as it was all we had to dig with. Some only got it about 2 feet Deep and them rappd the Dead Boddies up in our Bed Blankets and Placed them in the grave then covered them up. A few Days later Charley Cringo thaught it Best for Part of the out fit to go Back to the Panhandle to save exspences. So Bob Roberson taken one waggon and Part of the Boys named as follows C.W. Polk, James East, Lee Smith, Louis Boseman, Monroe Harriss, Billy McKay Tom Emery and Bob Williams. So we all

39

The Capture of Billy the Kid

started and left Charley there with the Balance of the Boys to gather cattle and Bring them Back as soon as spring opened up.

We puled out thrue the snow toworge the Panhandle. We would hafto melt snow to get watter for our horses to Drink. The second Day after we left the White Oaks we met a freight wagon loaded with whisky coming Las Vasgas

and in five minets we wer all over the waggon Driving nale holes in the Barrels and Downing the Red stuff out in tin buckets while the Driver stud and looked at us with menny thaughts, But said nothing. And when we got all we wanted he Drove on. We was all Dead Broke and had got mean and cared for nothing.

That night we come to a big tank. The man that oned it charged 10 cents a bucket for watter and 25 cents to watter horses. We wattered up again then filled up our Barrel as it was cheap. When we got Ready to start the oner come Down an counted it all up. It was 10 Dollars so as we had no monnie we just give him a check on the Peopels Bank of Ft. Ellitt Tx. Of corse they was no Bank there of that name.

So we started on happy and after travling all Day half Drunk on the Red eye. We struck camp and hobbled the horses all out cept mine. Kept him up to hunt them on the

Cal Polk

Cal Polk (left) served as a U.S. deputy marshal and later as city marshal of Holdenville, Oklahoma. (Courtesy of Mr. and Mrs. Edgar L. McVicker)

next morning. I taken there trails in the snow. After going about 2 miles I found them tide to a Big hay stack. The man that oned it charged 50 cents a peace for the Damage they had Done. I told him that was all Right so we started to the lot where they was tide. When we got to the lot I told him the Booss ho was at camp had all the monnie and that I would take the horses to camp and Bring the monnie back he wheeled around and said no the horses cant go un-

The Capture of Billy the Kid

til the monnie comes and started to the house. I drew my gun. I new we had no monnie at camp. I told him to stop and untie them horses in one minnet or I would Kill him. He stoped and tooked for a moment. I told him we had no monnie But had to have our horses and to untie them quick as I was in a hury.

He said it looked hard But he recond it was Best and when the last horse was untide I started the Bunch in a high Run toworge camp so I could get one a hill Before he got Back to the house. We started on and after travling about 7 miles we come to a sheep camp and Broke it up By taking every thing that was wanted such as Blankets, coffee, meat & Son. We went on and fiendly come to a small Mexacan Plazer which contained 2 stores and a saloon. Of corse we all stoped at the saloon and while we was getting Down Uncle Jimie Run in & slaped the Bartender in the face with his hat and told him to Bamos and out the greezer went at the Back Door. Uncle Jimmie then got a hand ax and nocked in the heads of 2 whisky Barrels. The Boys all got tin cups and Began Drinking the Red stuff like watter.

And of corse it took us 2 Days to get a way from there so we could straiting our selves up a gain for Buysness a gain. We then pulled out for the Panhandle and when we got to another mexacan Plazer By the name of

Troheo. While there that night I was looking over a nuse paper. I saw where Alf Polk ho was a Relation of mine had Killed two men in Westlasanamous, Colorado and was in Jale at that Place. I wrote him a letter asking him a Bout his trouble.

In too Days more we landed in Tascosa and there we all got on a Big Spree as our credit was good at old Jack Rynes Saloon. While there after every thing was full of Red licker. Bob Roberson got up on a center table to make a speach and while he was speaking, some one shuck the table and Down it came. Just at that time a man By the name of Cayho Jumped up and struck at Bob. Then it tuck all the Boys Busy for sometime to keep Bob from Killing Cayho. After every thing got quite, we found our way to camp which was close by and went to Bed. We got up the next morning and Pulled out for the LX Ranch. We got there at about 4 oclock in the evening.

THE
EARLY WEST

The Capture of Billy the Kid

George Coe, a close friend of Billy the Kid, as he appeared in about 1930. He lost his trigger finger in a shootout with Buckshot Roberts at Blazer's Mill in 1878.

Introduction to Louis Bousman Version

The following interview was found in Oklahoma City, Oklahoma, in a box of miscellaneous papers at an estate sale by a dealer of paper collectibles. I purchased it from him in Canton, Texas, as I helped the dealer unpack his wares.

Louis Bousman probably dictated this account while he was a part of the promotion of Johnny Mack Brown's movie version of the life of Billy the Kid. In Wichita Falls, Texas, in 1937, Bousman would have been viewed as a relic of the wild west.

Even though he was involved in two of the old West's most notable events—the capture of Billy the Kid and the big shootout at Tascosa, Louis Bousman disappeared from printed history. Publishing his story may bring forth more information about his later life. Hopefully it will help me find out why Bousman was known by the nickname "The Animal," which is the only way he is listed in some versions of the capture of Billy at Stinking Springs.

Jim Curry
Sulphur Springs, Texas
April, 1988

45

The Capture of Billy the Kid

Billy Wilson, who was captured with Billy the Kid on December 23, 1880, at Stinking Springs.

Louis Bousman

LOUIS BOUSMAN VERSION

REMINISCENSES OF LOUIS BOUSMAN

Wichita Falls, Texas. September 7, 1934

. . . .

I was born in the state of Virginia seventy-six years ago. I lived there until I was a good sized boy and then moved to Missouri, where I lived until after the Civil War. Then I moved to Grayson County, Texas, when I was about fourteen years old. Later I went to Cherokee Nation, close to Fort Gibson, and stayed a number of years. When I was about twenty years old, I moved to a place called Tascosa, in the Panhandle of Texas.

47

The Capture of Billy the Kid

At Tascosa, I worked for a cattle man named Lit Littlefield. The town was a wild and wooly place and everybody carried guns. I built a picket corrall out of cedar north of the Frying Pan Ranch in 1877. We killed buffalo right where the town of Amarillo now stands. Tascosa was forty-five miles northwest of Amarillo. The old Court House belongs to Mr. Rivens, a cow man who now lives in Amarillo. It is used as a ranch house. He owns the LIT ranch, which is about ten miles square.

The cattle men around Tascosa complained that the cowboys were stealing their cattle, and also the boys were striking for higher wages. The cow men got Pat Garrett to go down to Austin and get authority to put in a bunch of rangers and they put in four under Pat Garrett. But Pat didn't stay with them; he was sheriff in Lincoln County, New Mexico. Me and another Deputy Sheriff told the cow men that if they would go and swear out a warrant for these boys we would go out and arrest them. They did not do this. They were afraid of them. They thought that if they could get rid of them they would be all right. They wanted to make an agreement with us to stay in bed on a certain night while they hung the strikers. We told them that if they came in to kill the boys the fight would open, for we would protect the boys.

The "Home Rangers" didn't do a thing. They never

Louis Bousman

arrested a man. They wanted to run over everybody around town, so one night we got in a fight with them and killed three of them. Ed King was the first one that got killed, and then Fred Shelton, and I forget the other one's name, and one got away. I was Deputy Sheriff and one of our men got wounded, - a man named Len Woodruff. Me and a fellow they called "Cat Fish" never got a scratch. They buried the dead men out in what is called "Boot Hill Cemetary." They said I killed some of them. They shot Jessie Sheets and thought they were getting me. I heard a man say "I have got Bousman." They first started the row; they commenced the shooting and we shot back and blew some of their heads off. Pat Garrett was not there when the shooting took place. But they never put any more Rangers there after that.

"BILLY THE KID"

Billy was fourteen year old when he killed his first man in Silver City, New Mexico. He was a porter and general boot black around the hotel. He came from New York or somewhere in the east. There was a fellow there in the hotel who kept deviling Billy, and Billy told him that if he

49

The Capture of Billy the Kid

did not let him alone, he would kill him. The next morning the fellow commenced deviling him again and grabbed a hold of him, - so Billy killed him. Then he went out and stole him a horse and left and went down on the Pecos River where Chisolm's outfit was, and joined them. He hired to Chisolm as a cowboy and then Chisolm gave him five dollars a head for killing men. The Lincoln County war was going on. It was a cow men's war. They were fighting over the grazing land for cattle. Chisholm wanted it all. The war lasted about a year. After the war, Billy the Kid did not surrender. The government of New Mexico pardoned all these men, but Billy did not surrender to them.

Billy came to Tascosa in the Panhandle. He stayed at my camp a month. He stayed all around there among the cow men until Spring and then went back to New Mexico. Then he went to stealing cattle, - would come over south of Tascosa and get them and drive them away. The cow men got tired of it and got Pat Garrett to come over there and talk to him. Pat was sheriff of Lincoln County, and he told them that if they would send him bunch of men over there that he would capture Billy. I was one of the men sent over there and the others were Jim East, Tom Emory, Lon Chambers and Charles Siringo. And we had a Mexican cook with us. So we met up with Pat Garrett at Anton Chico in New Mexico. Then he picked out his men—pick-

Louis Bousman

Frank Clifford, alias Bigfoot Wallace, rode with Charley Siringo in search of the rustlers.

ed me and Jim East, Lon Chambers and Tom Emory, then he started down to Fort Sumner and rode all night. When we got there we sent a spy into Sumner in the day time to see if Billy and his bunch were there. So the spy stayed until dusk and then started back to meet us. He said, "When I left there, Billy and his men were there, Billy and his men were there in the town." So we rode into Fort Sumner before day and went to Pete Maxwell's barn, and thought we would find Billy's horses there. They were not there so we put our horses in the barn and went over town and saw that he was gone. So we got us a house and stayed inside— all but Pat Garrett and another man. Then Billy found out that we were there and sent a spy in to see who was

The Capture of Billy the Kid

there. The spy reported that Pat Garrett was there and one other white man and the rest were Mexicans. Billy and his gang were staying in a ranch house. The spy went back and told them we were there, and Billy sent him back that evening to see if he could find any more. Billy said, "I will just go down and run them out of town and dismount them." So he sent two men and Tom O'Philliard. He rode up to the hospital and Pat Garrett was standing there in the shade on the porch. And Pat said "Tom, throw up your hands." Tom reached down for his gun and Pat shot him. His horse went off with him and then he came back, and we went out and got him and carried him inside. Billy the Kid and three other men were watching from a distance, and we opened fire on them; so they left and went back out to the ranch house.

We buried Tom O'Philliard the next day. Billy sent a spy in there to see who all we were, and he told him who we were and that we were not all Mexicans. The spy came back and told us that if we would start out they would meet us half way. After we buried O'Philliard, we started out there that night, and the spy met us and said they were gone. We went to the house and took the trail of the horses and trailed them to the rock house and saw the horses tied on the outside. So me and Pat Garrett and Lon Chambers and a Mexican went over there and lay down in

52

Tascosa Texas
Thursday Oct 24th
1878

Know all persons by these presents
that I do hereby Sell and diliver
to Henry F. Hoyt one Sorrel
Horse Branded BB on left hip
and other indistinct Brands on
Shoulder for the Sum of Seventyfive
dollars. in hand Recieved

Witness   W H Bonney
Jos E McMasters
Geo J Howard.

This bill of sale was drawn up and signed by Billy the Kid on October 26th, 1878, for transferring ownership of a sorrel horse from the Kid to Henry F. Hoyt.

a hollow by the door so we could look in the door. We lay there all night in the snow on our blankets. And then Pat told us, "If Billy goes out to feed the horses, he will have on a Mexican hat. You boys cut down and kill him." Then Bowdre came out to feed the horses, so we all took a shot at him. He fell with his head back in the house. We thought it was Billy the Kid. Afterwards Bill hollered and said Bowdre wanted to come out there to us. Pat told him to come ahead and leave his guns in the house. But he

53

The Capture of Billy the Kid

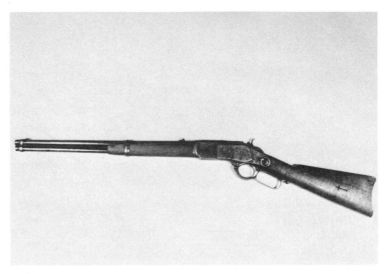

This 1873 Winchester (SN 47,629) was taken from Billy Wilson by Garrett, who carried it throughout the remainder of his career.

came out with his gun right in front of him with his hands up. And when he got out there, I raised up and got him and laid him down on my blanket. He was shot in three places and was bleeding. He did not live but a few minutes.

Billy and his outfit began trying to dig port holes in that rock house. There was only one north window and one west door. Pat says, "There is no use for us to lay here all day, we better get away from here before they do get port holes." Then we went down in the hollow a little ways and single filed across to where our horses were and

Louis Bousman

Colt Frontier (SN 55,093) that Garrett took from Billy Wilson at Stinking Springs. Garrett used this gun to kill Billy the Kid on July 14, 1881, at Fort Sumner.

the rest of the men. Then we went back to the ranch house and got us some breakfast. Billy and his bunch tried to lead their horses into the house. They were tied to a post, and they could reach out and get them. I shot the first one right in the neck and he fell with his shoulders right in the door. The next one Pat shot the rope in two, and he ran off and some of our bunch caught him. We got the ranchman to bring us down some food and some horse feed and we stayed all day, and finally Billy turned his horses out of the house in the middle of the evening

The Capture of Billy the Kid

and we got them. Between sun down and dusk Billy surrendered. He said he smelt that bacon frying and he was right hungry. We took them back to the ranch house and guarded them all night, and the dead man too. Then we pulled out to Fort Sumner with them the next morning. When we were getting right at Fort Sumner, Bowdre's wife came out to meet us in the snow. We whipped up the horses when we passed her and ran right up to the door, and I and Jim East grabbed the body and took it in and put it on the table. We didn't stop when we met her because we did not want to hear her abuse. She cussed Pat Garrett out. He told her to go over and pick out a suit of clothes to bury her husband in and he would pay for it. He also had the grave dug.

We kept Billy the Kid and the three others in his bunch, put them in a house and kept them under guard until the next morning and Pat pulled out with them to Las Vegas, New Mexico. He got in there at night and the people found out that he had Billy the Kid in jail and a mob tried to take him away from Pat, and he told them if they did not stand back he would arm Billy the Kid and his bunch and they could fight it out. Pat and four other men took the prisoners to Silver City, New Mexico and put them in jail there. They took him back to Lincoln afterwards where he was tried and got death sentence.

56

Louis Bousman

Charles Bowdre was killed by Garrett's posse when he was mistaken for the Kid at Stinking Springs.

After he got his sentence, they placed two guards over him. One morning one guard had gone to breakfast, the other was reading the newspaper, and Billy was standing behind him and hit him over the head with his hand cuffs. The guard started to run down stairs and Billy grabbed his gun from his scabbard and killed him. He then went back in the room and got a shot gun loaded with 22 buck shot and went down stairs and raised the window and saw the other guard coming and when he got right up close to him Billy hollered, "Look out! I am going to put them buck shot into you," and he killed him dead. Then Billy went back up stairs and armed himself with a winchester and

The Capture of Billy the Kid

six-shooters, ordered a Mexican to steal a horse for him that was right in behind the house where he was being guarded. He told him to bring the horse to the blacksmith shop. He had the blacksmith to cut his shackles in two. When Billy mounted the horse, the horse threw him. He ordered the Mexican to catch him, which he did, and Billy rode off. He went back to Fort Sumner and a month or two after that Pat Garrett killed him there at Pete Maxwell's house. Pat slipped into Maxwell's room and found out Billy was there. Billy overheard somebody talking, and he went to Maxwell's room, and he says "Maxwell what is that laying out here under these rose bushes?" Maxwell didn't answer, and then Pat shot him. That was John Poe, the deputy, lying out under the rose bushes. Billy was stuck on Maxwell's sister, the reason he went to their house, but Maxwell wanted to get rid of him.

The months of November and December of 1880 during which the Kid was pursued and captured by Garrett.

NOVEMBER 1880

SUN	MON	TUES	WED	THUR	FRI	SAT
	1	2	3	4	5	6
7	8	9	10	11	12	13
14	15	16	17	18	19	20
21	22	23	24	25	26	27
28	29	30				

DECEMBER 1880

SUN	MON	TUES	WED	THUR	FRI	SAT
			1	2	3	4
5	6	7	8	9	10	11
12	13	14	15	16	17	18
19	20	21	22	23	24	25
26	27	28	29	30	31	

The Capture of Billy the Kid

Charles W. Foor standing in front of a cave used as a hideout by the Kid.

3

CHARLES W. FOOR
MAP OF FT. SUMNER

Charles W. Foor was a lifelong resident of the Fort Sumner area who assisted those wanting to find the sites and locations of the exploits of Billy the Kid and Pat Garrett. A previously unpublished map of Fort Sumner, that was drawn by Foor, is given on the following pages.

This map was drawn on a 30 inch X 36 inch panel of gypsum wallboard in ink and tinted with pastel shades of watercolors. Over the past sixty years the map has faded, but it can be clearly read and interpreted. It has been exactly traced to make the copy a facsimile of the original that would reproduce satisfactorily for this book.

On the map itself, Foor states that he came to Fort Sumner in October of 1881, three months after Garrett killed the Kid. Some historians claim that Foor was living in Fort Sumner at the time of the killing, and that he was one of the pallbearers at the Kid's burial. Considering his interest in Fort Sumner history, it is unlikely that Charley would have incorrectly reported this date.

This map represents another rare first hand description of the principal area of the Kid/Garrett legend that was drawn by an observer who was THERE.

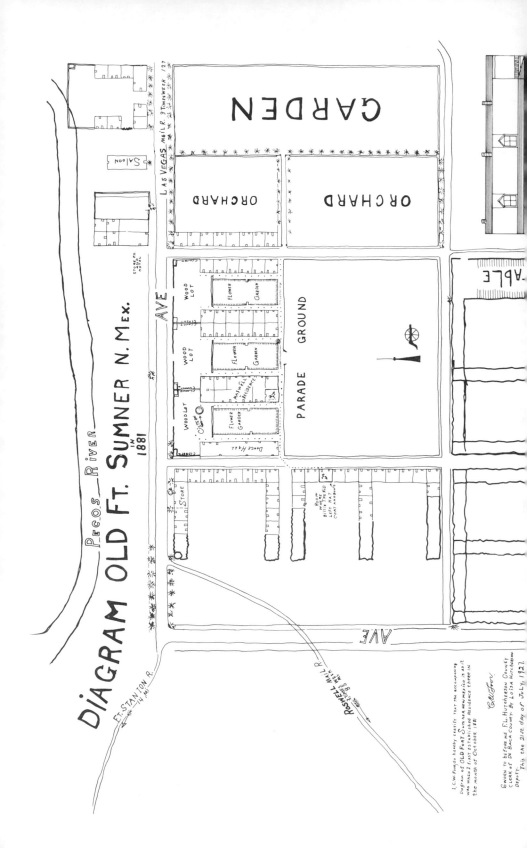

DIAGRAM OLD FT. SUMNER N. MEX.
IN
1881

PECOS RIVER

FT. STANTON R. 14 MI

LAS VEGAS MAIL R. 3 TIMES WEEK 127

GARDEN

ORCHARD

ORCHARD

SALOON

STONE R.O.
HOTEL

AVE

WOOD LOT

FLOWER GARDEN

WOOD LOT

FLOWER GARDEN

WOOD LOT

CISTERN

FLOWER GARDEN

MAXWELL RESIDENCE

DANCE HALL

PARADE GROUND

STORE

ROOM WHERE BILLIE THE KID LEFT WAY COAT HANGING

STABLE

AVE

ROSWELL MAIL R. 3 TIMES WEEK

I, C. W. FRENCH hereby certify that the accompanying Diagram of OLD FORT SUMNER NEW MEXICO is as it was when I first established Residence there in the month of October 1881

SWORN TO before me F. L. HUTCHERSON COUNTY CLERK OF DE BACA COUNTY. By LOISA HUTCHERSON DEPUTY.
This the 21st day of JULY, 1927.

Front View of The MAXWELL RESIDENCE

Hospital

BLANCO, R.O.
Tex. R
/Timberweek 1793

ADOBE WALLS →
OLD RUINS
PARADE GROUND AND COTTON WOOD TREES →
WALKWAY
DITCHES →
ROADS →

INHABITED BUILDINS

OLD NAVAJO CORRAL

DITCH

LAKE

CEMETERY

The Capture of Billy the Kid

THE KILLING OF TOM O'FOLLIARD

Charles Foor did not mark his map to show where Tom O'Folliard had been killed. However, the editor has enlarged Foor's map of the hospital area and has indicated where the encounter probably occurred on December 19, 1880.

Garrett's posse had entered Fort Sumner while the Kid and his gang were at the Wilcox ranch about twelve miles away. The Kid had left spies in Fort Sumner to observe the actions of Garrett. Pat sent a falsified note by a local Mexican to the Wilcox ranch reporting that the posse had left for Roswell. The plan worked and the Kid's gang rode toward Fort Sumner in the snow to celebrate. Garrett had occupied the hospital building where Bowdre's wife lived and where the gang was expected to come. Several of the posse members were stationed outside the building and the rest played poker inside and waited.

At about eight o'clock the Kid's gang was spotted by a lookout. Garrett's men positioned themselves, and when they were in range, Garrett shouted, "Halt!"

O'Folliard reached for his gun and drew the fire from Garrett and his men while the rest of the Kid's gang fled into the darkness. Tom soon fell from his horse and died within the hour in the hospital building while in the custody of Garrett's posse.

O'Folliard was buried at the Fort Sumner cemetery.

64

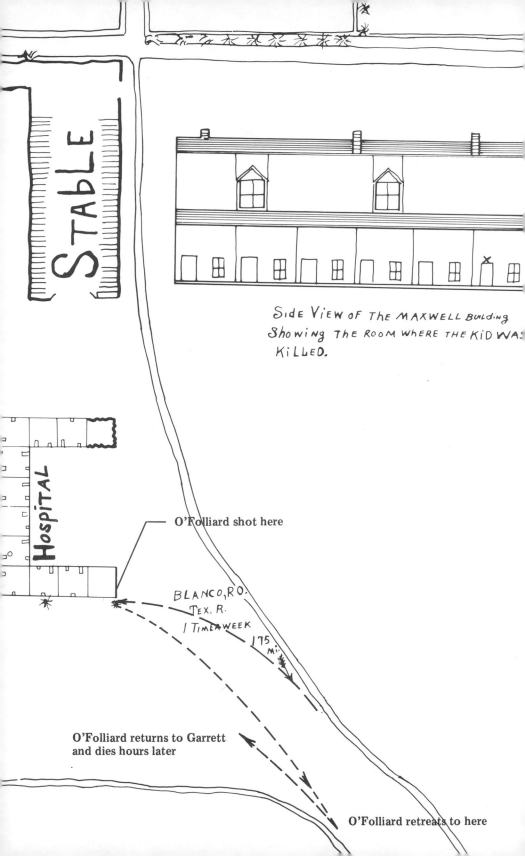

STABLE

SIDE VIEW OF THE MAXWELL Building Showing THE ROOM WHERE THE KID WAS KILLED.

HOSPITAL

O'Folliard shot here

BLANCO, RO.
TEX. R.
1 TIME A WEEK
175 MI.

O'Folliard returns to Garrett
and dies hours later

O'Folliard retreats to here

The Capture of Billy the Kid

THE KILLING OF THE KID

Charles Foor marked the route the Kid took from his room to Pete Maxwell's. These were his final steps into immortality. Receiving a tip that the Kid was in Fort Sumner Sheriff Pat Garrett and Deputies John Poe and Tip McKinney arrived there before sundown. The lawmen waited in a peach orchard until dark to remain undetected by the townspeople.

About 11:30 p.m. on July 14, 1881, Garrett went to Pete Maxwell's room, leaving Poe and McKinney on the porch outside.

Meanwhile, as if drawn by destiny, the Kid left Celsa Gutierrez's room to cut a piece of meat from a beef hanging on the porch of Maxwell's house. Half-dressed and carrying a butcher knife and revolver, he was startled when he noticed Poe and McKinney in the shadows. Billy backed into Pete's room—where Pat Garrett was sitting on the bed in the dark—and asked, "Quien es? Who are they, Pete?"

Recognizing Billy's voice, Pat drew his gun and fired two shots at the Kid. The first one struck Billy in the heart, killing him instantly. Garrett hurried to the porch where Poe and McKinney were crouching with guns drawn. After a few moments, it was apparent that the Kid was dead.

After a coroner's inquest was held, Billy the Kid was buried in the Fort Sumner cemetery, next to his two friends, Charles Bowdre and Tom O'Folliard.

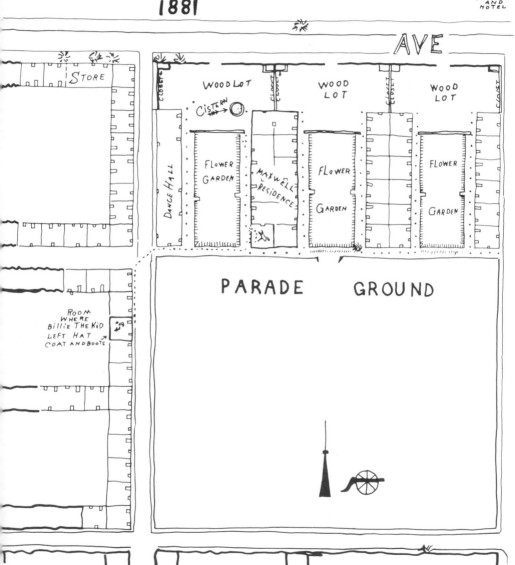

PECOS RIVER

D FT. SUMNER N. MEX.

IN 1881

STORE P.O AND HOTEL

AVE

STORE

WOOD LOT

CISTERN

CLOSET

WOOD LOT

CLOSET

WOOD LOT

CLOSET

DANCE HALL

FLOWER GARDEN

MAXWELL RESIDENCE

FLOWER GARDEN

FLOWER GARDEN

ROOM WHERE BILLIE THE KID LEFT HAT COAT AND BOOTS

PARADE   GROUND

67

The Capture of Billy the Kid

A photograph of Charles A. Siringo that was inscribed to historian E. A. Brininstool on December 28, 1927.

SIRINGO/EAST VERSION

Charley Siringo did not go to Stinking Springs with Pat Garrett's posse to capture Billy the Kid and his gang. Siringo did obtain a letter from Jim East who gave his firsthand version of the shootout at Stinking Springs which was included in Siringo's book, THE HISTORY OF BILLY THE KID.

The chapter from this book in which Jim East's letter was reproduced is included in the pages that follow, thus adding another remembrance of one of the participants.

THE HISTORY OF BILLY THE KID was published in 1920 by Charles A. Siringo. It has since become a rare collector's item which is difficult to obtain.

The Capture of Billy the Kid

"BILLY THE KID" ADDS ONE MORE NOTCH TO HIS GUN AS A KILLER. TRAPPED AT LAST BY PAT GARRETT AND POSSE. TWO OF HIS GANG KILLED. IN JAIL AT SANTA FE.

In the year 1879, rich gold ore had been struck on Baxter mountain, three miles from White Oaks Spring, about thirty miles north of Lincoln, and the new town of White Oak was established, with a population of about one thousand souls.

The "Kid" had many friends in the hurrah mining camp. He had shot up the town, and was wanted by the law officers.

On the 23rd day of November, 1880, the "Kid" celebrated his birthday in White Oaks, under cover, among friends.

On riding out of town with his gang after dark, he took one friendly shot at Deputy Sheriff Jim Woodland, who was standing in front of the Pioneer Saloon. The chances are he had no intention of shooting Woodland, as he was a warm friend to his chum, Tom O'Phalliard, who was riding by his side. O'Phalliard and Jim Woodland had come to New Mexico from Texas together, a few years previous. Woodland is still a resident of Lincoln County, with a permanent home on the large Block cattle ranch.

This shot woke up Deputy Sheriffs Jim Carlyle and J. N. Bell, who fired parting shots at the gang, as they galloped out of town.

70

The next day a posse was made up of leading citizens of White Oaks with Deputy Sheriff Will Hudgens and Jim Carlyle in command. They followed the trail of the outlaw gang to Coyote Spring, where they came onto the gang in camp. Shots were exchanged. "Billy the Kid" had sprung onto his horse, which was shot from under him.

When the "Kid's" gang fired on the posse, Johnny Hudgens' mount fell over dead, shot in the head.

The weather was bitter cold and snow lay on the ground. Without overcoat or gloves, "Billy the Kid" rushed for the hills, afoot, after his horse fell. The rest of the gang had become separated, and each one looked out for himself.

In the outlaws' camp the posse found a good supply of grub and plunder.

Jim Carlyle appropriated the "Kids" gloves and put them on his hands. No doubt they were the real cause of his death later.

With "Billy the Kid's" saddle, overcoat and the other plunder found in the outlaws' camp, the posse returned to White Oaks, arriving there about dark.

It would seem from all accounts that "Billy the Kid" trailed the posse into White Oaks, where he found shelter at the Dedrick and West Livery Stable. He was seen on the street during the night.

On November 27th, a posse of White Oaks citizens under command of Jim Carlyle and Will Hudgens, rode to the Jim Greathouse road-ranch, about forty miles north,

The Capture of Billy the Kid

arriving there before daylight. Their horses were secreted, and they made breastworks of logs and brush so as to cover the ranch house, which was known to be a rendezvous of the "Kid's" gang.

After daylight the cook came out of the house with a nosebag and ropes to hunt the horses which had been hobbled the evening before.

This cook, Steck, was captured by the posse behind the breastworks. He confessed that the "Kid" and his gang were in the house.

Now Steck was sent to the house with a note to the "Kid" demanding his surrender. The reply he sent back by Steck read: "You can only take me a corpse."

The proprietor of the ranch, Jim Greathouse, accompanied Steck back to the posse behind the logs.

Jimmie Carlyle suggested that he go to the house unarmed and have a talk with the "Kid." Will Hudgens wouldn't agree to this until after Greathouse said he would remain to guarantee Carlyle's safe return. That if the "Kid" should kill Carlyle, they could take his life.

A time limit was set for Carlyle's return, or Greathouse would be killed. This was written on a note and sent by Steck to the "Kid."

When Carlyle entered the saloon, in the front part of the log building, the "Kid" greeted him in a friendly manner, but seeing his gloves sticking out of Carlyle's coat pocket, he grabbed them saying: "What in the h—l are you doing with my gloves?" Of course this brought back the

This photograph is believed by many to be that of Billy the Kid.

The Capture of Billy the Kid

misery he had endured without gloves after the posse raided their camp at Coyote Spring.

Here he invited Carlyle up to the bar to take his last drink on earth—as he said he intended to kill him when the whiskey was down.

After Carlyle had drained his glass the "Kid" pulled his pistol and told him to say his prayers before he fired.

With a laugh the "Kid" put up his pistol, saying, "Why Jimmie, I wouldn't kill you. Let's all take another friendly drink."

Now the time was spent singing and dancing. Every time the gang took a drink, Carlyle had to join them in a social glass.

The "Kid" afterwards told friends that he had no intention of killing Carlyle, that he just wanted to detain him till after dark, so they could make a dash for liberty.

The time had just expired when the posse were to kill Jim Greathouse, if Carlyle was not back. At that moment a man behind the breastworks fired a shot at the house. Carlyle supposed this shot had killed Greathouse, which would result in his own death. He leaped for the glass window, taking sash and all with him. The "Kid" fired a bullet into him. When he struck the ground he began crawling away on his hands and knees, as he was badly wounded. Now the "Kid" finished him with a well aimed shot from his pistol.

The men behind the logs were witnesses to this murder,—as they could see Carlyle crawling away from the window. Now they opened fire with a vengeance on the building. The gang had previously piled sacks of grain and flour against the doors, to keep out the bullets.

In the excitement, Jim Greathouse slipped away from the posse and ran through the woods. Finding one of his own hobbled ponies, he mounted him and rode away. He was later shot by deperado Joe Fowler, with a double-barrel shot gun, as he lay in bed asleep. This murder took place on Joe Fowler's cattle ranch west of Socorro, New Mexico.

After dark the posse concluded to return to White Oaks, as they were cold and hungry. They had brought no grub with them, and they dared not build a fire to keep warm, for fear of being shot by the gang.

A few hours later the "Kid" and gang made a break for liberty, intending to fight the posse to a finish, they not knowing that the officers had departed.

All night the gang waded through the deep snow, afoot. They arrived at Mr. Spence's ranch at daylight, and ate a hearty breakfast. Then continued their journey towards Anton Chico on the Pecos river.

About daylight that morning, Will Hudgens, Johnny Hurley, and Jim Brent made up a large posse and started to the Greathouse road-ranch. Arriving there, they found the place vacated. The buildings were set afire, then the journey continued on the gang's trail, in the deep snow.

A highly respected citizen, by the name of Spence, had established a road-ranch on a cut-off road between

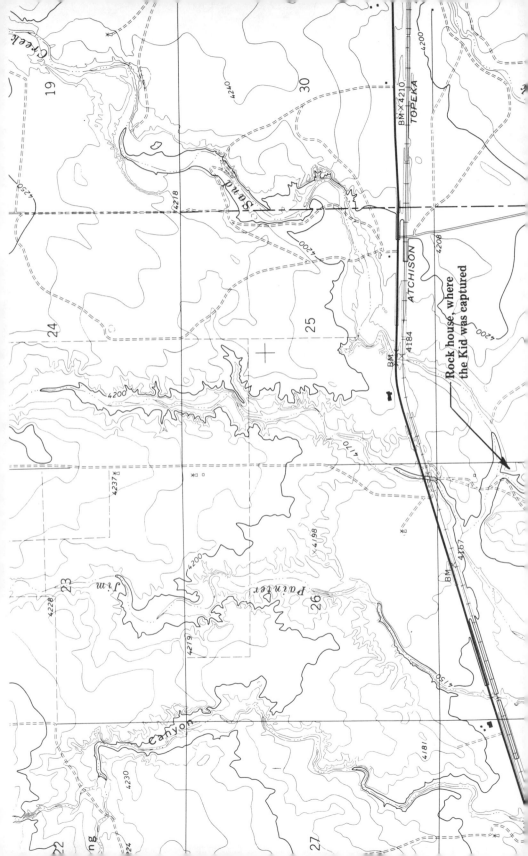

Rock house, where
the Kid was captured

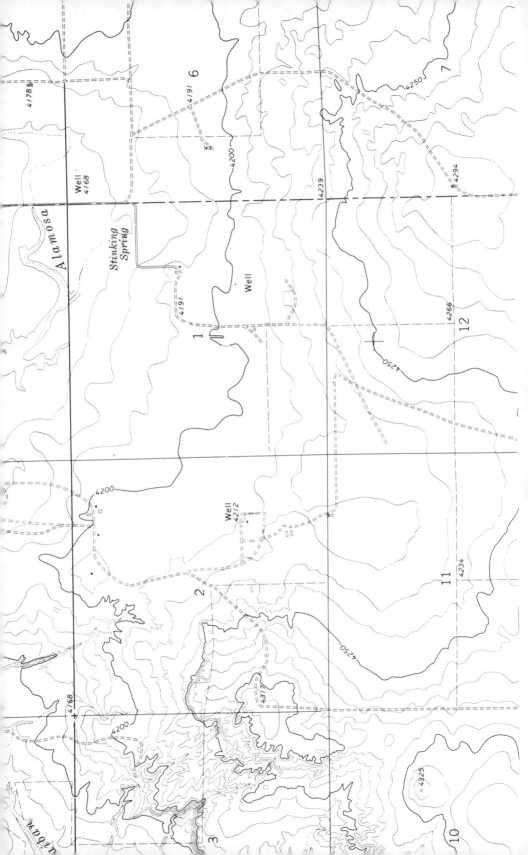

The Capture of Billy the Kid

White Oaks and Las Vegas. The gang's trail led up to this ranch, and Mr. Spence acknowledged cooking breakfast for them.

Now Mr. Spence was dragged to a tree with a rope around his neck to hang him. Many of the posse protested against the hanging of Spence, and his life was spared, but revenge was taken by burning his buildings.

The "Kid's" trail was now followed into a rough, hilly country and there abandoned. Then the posse returned to White Oaks.

In Anton Chico, the "Kid" and his party stole horses and saddles, and rode down the Pecos river.

A few days later, Pat Garrett, the sheriff of Lincoln County, arrived in Anton Chico from Fort Sumner, to make up a posse to run down the "Kid" and his gang.

At this time the writer and Bob Roberson had arrived in Anton Chico from Tascosa, Texas, with a crew of fighting cowboys, to help run down the "Kid," and put a stop to the stealing of Panhandle, Texas, cattle.

The author had charge of five "warriors," Jas. H. East, Cal Polk, Lee Hall, Frank Clifford (Big-Foot Wallace), and Lon Chambers. We were armed to the teeth, and had four large mules to draw the mess-wagon, driven by the Mexican cook, Francisco.

Bob Roberson was in charge of five riders and a mess-wagon.

At our camp, west of Anton Chico, Pat Garrett met us, and we agreed to loan him a few of our "warriors." The writer turned over to him three men, Jim East, Lon Chambers and Lee Hall. Bob Roberson turned over to him three cowboys, Tom Emmory, Bob Williams, and Louis Bozeman.

We then continued our journey to White Oaks in a raging snow storm.

Pat Garrett started down the Pecos river with his crew, consisting of our six cowboys, his brother-in-law, Barney Mason, and Frank Stewart, who had been acting as detective for the Panhandle cattlemen's association.

At Fort Sumner, Pat Garrett deputized Charlie Rudolph and a few Mexican friends, to join the crowd which now numbered about thirteen men.

Finding that the "Kid" and party had been in Fort Sumner, and made the old abandoned United States Hospital building, where lived Charlie Bowdre and his half-breed Mexican wife, their headquarters, Pat Garrett concluded to camp there. He figured that the outlaws would return and visit Mrs. Charlie Bowdre, whose husband was one of the outlaw band.

In order to get a true record of the capture of "Billy the Kid" and gang, the author wrote to James H. East, of Douglas, Arizona, for the facts. Jim East is the only known living participant in that tragic event. His reputation for honesty and truthfulness is above par wherever he is known. He served eight years as sheriff of Oldham County, Texas, at Tascosa, and was city marshal for several years in Douglas, Arizona.

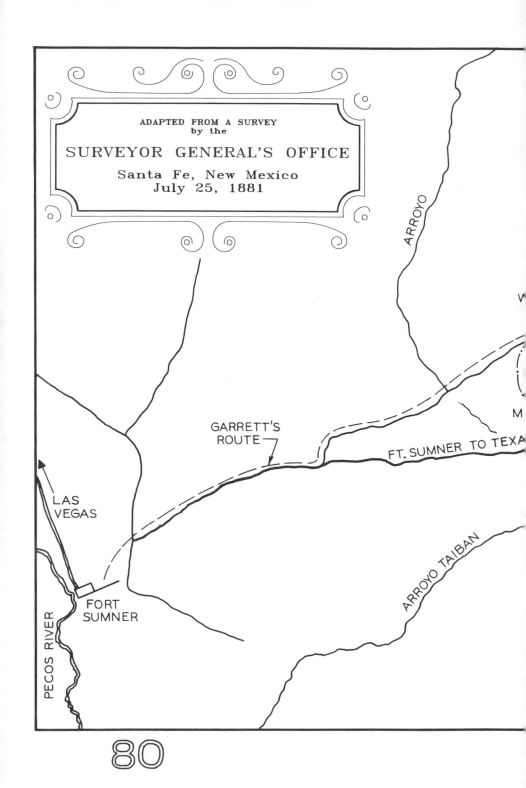

ADAPTED FROM A SURVEY
by the

SURVEYOR GENERAL'S OFFICE

Santa Fe, New Mexico
July 25, 1881

ARROYO

GARRETT'S
ROUTE

FT. SUMNER TO TEXA

LAS
VEGAS

ARROYO TAIBAN

PECOS RIVER

FORT
SUMNER

80

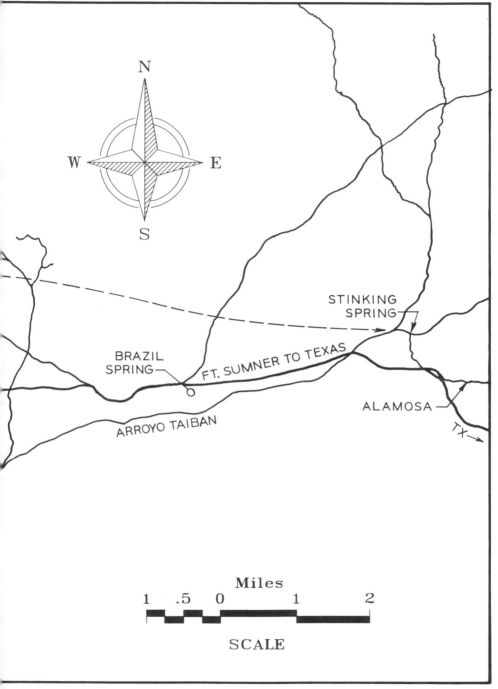

N

W   E

S

STINKING
SPRING

BRAZIL
SPRING

FT. SUMNER TO TEXAS

ALAMOSA

ARROYO TAIBAN

TX

Miles

1   .5   0   1   2

SCALE

81

The Capture of Billy the Kid

Herewith his letter to the writer is printed in full:

"Douglas, Arizona,
May 1st, 1920.

Dear Charlie:

Yours of the 29th received, and contents noted. I will try to answer your questions, but you know after a lapse of forty years, one's memory may slip a cog. First: We were quartered in the old Government Hospital building in Ft. Sumner, the night of the first fight. Lou Chambers was on guard. Our horses were in Pete Maxwell's stable. Sheriff Pat Garrett, Tom Emmory, Bob Williams, and Barney Mason were playing poker on a blanket on the floor.

I had just laid down on my blanket in the corner, when Chambers ran in and told us that the 'Kid' and his gang were coming. It was about eleven o'clock at night. We all grabbed our guns and stepped out in the yard.

Just then the 'Kid's' men came around the corner of the old hospital building, in front of the room occupied by Charlie Bowdre's woman and her mother. Tom O'Phalliard was riding in the lead. Garrett yelled out: 'Throw up your hands!" But O'Phalliard jerked his pistol. Then the shooting commenced. It being dark, the shooting was at random.

Tom O'Phalliard was shot through the body, near the heart, and lost control of his horse. 'Kid' and the rest of his men whirled their horses and ran up the road.

O'Phalliard's horse came up near us, and Tom said:

'Don't shoot any more, I am dying.' We helped him off his horse and took him in, and laid him down on my blanket. Pat and the other boys then went back to playing poker.

I got Tom some water. He then cussed Garrett and died, in about thirty minutes after being shot.

The horse that Dave Rudabaugh was riding was shot, but not killed instantly. We found the dead horse the next day on the trail, about one mile or so east of Ft. Sumner.

After Dave's horse fell down from loss of blood, he got up behind Billy Wilson, and they all went to Wilcox's ranch that night.

The next morning a big snow storm set in and put out their trail, so we laid over in Sumner and buried Tom O'Phalliard.

The next night, after the fight, it cleared off and about midnight, Mr. Wilcox rode in and reported to us that the "Kid," Dave Rudabaugh, Billy Wilson, Tom Pickett, and Charlie Bowdre, had eaten supper at his ranch about dark, then pulled out for the little rock house at Stinking Spring. So we saddled up and started about one o'clock in the morning.

We got to the rock house just before daylight. Our horses were left with Frank Stewart and some of the other boys under guard, while Garrett took Lee Hall, Tom Emory and myself with him. We crawled up the arroyo to within about thirty feet of the door, where we lay down in the snow.

There was no window in this house, and only one

The Capture of Billy the Kid

door, which we would cover with our guns.

The "Kid" had taken his race mare into the house, but the other three horses were standing near the door, hitched by ropes to the vega poles.

Just as day began to show, Charlie Bowdre came out to feed his horse. I suppose, for he had a moral in one hand. Garrett told him to throw up his hands, but he grabbed at his six-shooter. Then Garrett and Lee Hall both shot him in the breast. Emory and I didn't shoot, for there was no use to waste ammunition then.

Charlie turned and went into the house, and we heard the 'Kid' say to him: 'Charlie, you are done for. Go out and see if you can't get one of the s—of—b's before you die."

Charlie then walked out with his hand on his pistol, but was unable to shoot. We didn't shoot, for we could see he was about dead. He stumbled and fell on Lee Hall. He started to speak, but the words died with him.

Now Garrett, Lee, Tom and I, fired several shots at the ropes which held the horses, and cut them loose—all but one horse which was half way in the door. Garrett shot him down, and that blocked the door, so the 'Kid' could not make a wolf dart on his mare.

We then held a medicine talk with the Kid, but of course couldn't see him. Garrett asked him to give up, Billy answered: 'Go to h—l, you long-legged s—of a b!"

Garrett then told Tom Emory and I to go around to the other side of the house, as we could hear them trying

84

An early photograph of Jim East (front right) that was probably made in Tascosa, Texas, in the 1880s.

85

The Capture of Billy the Kid

to pick out a port-hole. Then we took it, time about, guarding the house all that day. When nearly sundown, we saw a white handkerchief on a stick, poked out of the chimney. Some of us crawled up the arroyo near enough to talk to 'Billy.' He said they had no show to get away, and wanted to surrender, if we would give our word not to fire into them, when they came out. We gave the promise, and they came out with their hands up, but that traitor, Barney Mason, raised his gun to shoot the 'Kid,' when Lee Hall and I covered Barney and told him to drop his gun, which he did.

Now we took the prisoners and the body of Charlie Bowdre to the Wilcox ranch, where we stayed until next day. Then to Ft. Sumner, where we delivered the body of Bowdre to his wife. Garrett asked Louis Bousman and I to take Bowdre in the house to his wife. As we started in with him, she struck me over the head with a branding iron, and I had to drop Charlie at her feet. The poor woman was crazy with grief. I always regretted the death of Charlie Bowdre, for he was a brave man, and true to his friends to the last.

Before we left Ft. Sumner with the prisoners for Santa Fe, the 'Kid' asked Garrett to let Tom Emory and I go along as guards, which, as you know, he did.

The 'Kid' made me a present of his Winchester rifle, but old Beaver Smith made such a roar about an account he said 'Billy' owed him, that at the request of 'Billy,' I gave old Beaver the gun. I wish now I had kept it.

Siringo/East

On the road to Santa Fe, the 'Kid' told Garrett this: That those who live by the sword, die by the sword. Part of that prophecy has come true. Pat Garrett got his, but I am still alive.

I must close. You may use any quotations from my letters, for they are true. Good luck to you. Mrs. East joins me in best wishes.

Sincerely yours,

JAS. H. EAST."

The author had previously written to Jim East about "Billy the Kid's " sweetheart, Miss Dulcinea del Toboso. Here is a quotation from his answer, of April 26th, 1920: "Your recollection of Dulcinea de Toboso, about tallies with the way I remember her. She was rather stout, built like her mother, but not so dark.

"After we captured 'Billy the Kid' at Arroyo Tivan, we took him, Dave Rudabaugh, Billy Wilson, and Tom Pickett—also the dead body of Charlie Bowdre—to Fort Sumner.

"After dinner Mrs. Toboso sent over an old Navajo woman to ask Pat Garrett to let 'Billy' come over to the house and see them before taking him to Santa Fe. So Garrett told Lee Hall and I to guard "Billy' and Dave Rudebough over to Toboso's, Dave and 'Billy' being shackled together. As we went over the lock on Dave's leg came loose, and 'Billy' being very superstitious, said: 'That is a bad sign. I will die, and Dave will go free,' which, as you know, proved true.

The Capture of Billy the Kid

When we went in the house only Mrs. Toboso, Dulcinea, and the old Navajo woman were there.

"Mrs. Toboso asked Hall and I to let 'Billy' and Dulcinea go into another room and talk awhile, but we did not do so, for it was only a stall of 'Billy's' to make a run for liberty, and the old lady and girl were willing to further the scheme. The lovers embraced, and she gave 'Billy' one of those soul kisses the novelists tell us about, till it being time to hit the trail for Vegas, we had to pull them apart, much against our wishes, for you know all the world loves a lover."

It was December 23rd, 1880, when the "Kid" and gang, Dave Rudebaugh, Tom Pickett and Billy Wilson—were captured, and Charlie Bowdre killed.

The prisoners were taken to the nearest railroad, at Las Vegas, where a mob tried to take them away from the posse, to string them up.

They were placed in the County jail at Santa Fe, the capital of the Territory of New Mexico, as the penitentiary was not yet completed.

Dave Rudebaugh was tried and sentenced to death for the killing of the jailer in Las Vegas. Later he made his escape and has never been heard of since.

THE
EARLY WEST

Rock house, where
the Kid was captured

*An aerial photograph of Stinking Springs that was taken
in 1983. (Courtesy of the U.S. Department of Interior.)*

5

PAT GARRETT VERSION

The following account of the capture of the Kid and his gang was written in Pat Garrett's book, THE AUTHENTIC LIFE OF BILLY THE KID, that was published in 1882 by New Mexico Printing and Publishing Company of Santa Fe, New Mexico. This book is described by bibliographer Ramon F. Adams as "exceedingly rare."

Most authorities agree that a portion of this book was written by, or with the assistance of, Ash Upson, Garrett's close friend who was present during most of Pat's career in Lincoln and Fort Sumner. Upson, a newspaperman, probably wrote and polished the story as it was told to him by Garrett.

With Garrett's following version, all the known first-hand versions of the Kid's capture at Stinking Springs are given in this volume.

The Capture of Billy the Kid

A Mob at Las Vegas Want Rudabaugh - The Kid in Jail
At Santa Fe - Attempt to Escape - The Kid on Trial
at Mesilla for Murder- Sentenced to Hang - Con-
fined at Lincoln

On the morning of the 18th of December, before anyone was stirring in the plaza of Fort Sumner, I left our party with the exception of Mason in concealment, and started out to make observations. I met a Mexican named Iginio Garcia in my rounds, whom I knew to be a tool of the Kid's, and I spoke to him. I warned him not to betray my presence to any of the Kid's gang and not to leave the plaza. He represented that he had urgent business down the river but assured me that he would keep my presence a secret. I consented for him to go, as it didn't matter much. If the Kid and his associates found out I was there, they would labor under the impression that my only support in the engagement would be Mason, and perhaps a Mexican or two. The fact of the presence of Stewart and his party I felt sure had not been betrayed to anyone. Garcia lived twelve miles south of Fort Sumner, and started in that direction.

A day or two previous to these events, A.H. Smith had sent Bob Campbell and Jose Valdez to Bosque Grande to drive up a bunch of milk cows which he had bought from Dan Dedrick. Garcia happened to meet these two near his home. He knew that Campbell was a friend and an accomplice of the Kid and that Valdez was, at least, a friend. He told them I was at Fort Sumner, and they immediately turned the cows loose and separated. Campbell at once went to a camp close by, hired a Mexican boy, and sent him to the Kid with a note. The Kid and his gang were then at the ranch of Erastus J. Wilcox, twelve miles east of Sumner.

Valdez rode into Sumner, and there, when I met him, I inquired if he had seen Garcia. He said he had seen him at a distance but had not spoken to him. I asked no further questions, as I was convinced I would get no word of truth from him. On receipt of Campbell's note, the Kid sent Juan, a stepson of Wilcox, to the Fort to see how the land lay and with instructions to return and report as soon as possible. Wilcox and his partner, Brazil, were law-abiding citizens, and subsequently rendered me invaluable assistance in my efforts to capture the gang. Seeing Juan in the plaza, I suspected his errand, accosted him, and found my surmise was correct. After a little conversation I concluded that I could fully trust him; and when I made known my business to him he promised faithfully to follow my instructions. From him I gathered the following information about the Kid's movements.

The Capture of Billy the Kid

The Kid and all his band were intending to come to Fort Sumner the next day in a wagon with a load of beef. That morning, however, the Kid had received by a Mexican boy a note from Bob Campbell wherein Bob told how he and Valdez met Garcia and how Garcia had notified them of my presence in Sumner. So from this I knew that Valdez had lied to me. This note had disarranged the Kid's plans. He had sent Juan in to try to learn something of my movements, the number in my posse, etc. I asked Juan if he would work with me to deceive the outlaws. He said he would do anything I told him. Thereupon I left him and went to Valdez. I made the latter write a note to the Kid saying that all my party and I had gone to Roswell and there was no danger. I then wrote a note to Wilcox and Brazil, stating that I was at Fort Sumner with thirteen men, that I was on the trail of the Kid and his gang, and that I would never let up until I caught them or ran them out of the country. I closed with the request that they co-operate with me. When Juan had finished his business in the plaza and came to me, I gave him the two notes, warning him not to get them mixed.

The Kid and his party were impatiently awaiting Juan's return. They read Valdez' note eagerly—then shouted their scorn at my timidity, saying that this news was too good for them; that they had intended to come in af-

94

ter me anyhow; that they had a great notion to follow me and my party; that if they could kill me they would not be further molested; and that if we had not run away they would have "shot us up a little" and set us on foot. Juan was discreet, and when opportunity arose, he gave the other note to Wilcox.

I was confident that the gang would be in Fort Sumner that night and made arrangements to receive them. There was an old hospital building on the eastern boundary of the plaza—the direction from which they would come. The wife of Bowdre occupied one of the rooms of the building, and I felt sure they would pay their first visit to her. So I took my posse there, placed a guard about the house, and awaited the game. They came fully two hours before we expected them. We were passing away the time playing cards. There were several Mexicans in the plaza, some of whom I feared would convey information to the gang, as I had them with me in custody. Snow was falling on the gound, the fact of which increased the light outside. About eight o'clock the guard cautiously called from the door,

"Pat, some one is coming!"

"Get your guns, boys," said I. "No one but the men we want would be riding at this time of night."

With all his reckless bravery, the Kid had a strong in-

The Capture of Billy the Kid

This illustration from Garrett's book, THE AUTHEN-
TIC LIFE OF BILLY THE KID, shows the Kid's gang
pinned down by Garrett's posse at Stinking Springs.

The Capture of Billy the Kid

fusion of caution in his composition when he was not excited. He afterwards told me that as they approached the building that night he was riding in front of O'Folliard. As they rode down close to our vicinity, he said a strong suspicion arose in his mind that they might be running into unseen danger.

"Well," said I, "what did you do?"

He replied—"I wanted a chew of tobacco bad. Wilson had some that was good and he was in the rear. I went back after tobacco, don't you see?" and his eyes twinkled mischievously.

One of the Mexicans followed me out, and we joined the guard, Lon Chambers, on one side of the building, while Mason with the rest of our party went around the building to intercept them should they try to pass on into the plaza. In a short time we saw the Kid's gang approaching, with O'Folliard and Pickett riding in front. I was under the porch and close against the wall, partly hidden by some harness hanging there. Chambers was close behind me, and the Mexican behind him. I whispered, "That's him." They rode on up until O'Folliard's horse's head was under the porch. When I called "Halt!" O'Folliard reached for his pistol, but before he could draw it, Chambers and I both fired. His horse wheeled and ran at least a hundred and fifty yards. As quick as possible I fired at Pickett, but the flash of Chambers' gun disconcerted my aim, and I missed him. But one might have thought by the way he ran and yelled that I had a dozen bullets in him. When O'Folliard's horse ran with him, he was uttering cries of mortal agony; and we were convinced that he had received a death wound. But he wheeled his horse, and as he rode slowly back, said, "Don't shoot, Garrett. I am killed."

Mason, from the other side of the house where he had been stationed, called out, "Take your medicine, old boy; take your medicine," and was going to O'Folliard's assistance. But fearing that it might be a feint and that O'Folliard might attempt revenge on Mason, I called out a warning to the latter to be careful how he approached the wounded man. Then I called to O'Folliard to throw up his hands, adding that I would give him no chance to kill me. He replied that he was dying and couldn't throw up his hands, and begged us to take him off his horse and let him die as easy as possible. Holding our guns down on him, we went up to him, took his gun out of the scabbard, lifted him off his horse, carried him into the house, and laid him down. Then taking off his pistol, which was full-cocked, we examined him and found that he was shot through the left side just below the heart, his coat having been cut across the front by a bullet.

During this encounter with O'Folliard and Pickett,

The Capture of Billy the Kid

Territorial governor Lew Wallace offered $500 reward for Billy the Kid. Wallace is better known for his book, BEN HUR.

the rest of our party on the other side of the house had seen the Kid and the others of his gang. My men had promptly fired on them and killed Rudabaugh's horse, which, however, ran twelve miles with him to Wilcox's ranch before the animal died. As soon as our men fired, these four ran like a bunch of wild Nueces steers. They were, in truth, completely surprised and demoralized.

As soon as the outlaws had disappeared Mason came around the building just as O'Folliard was returning, reeling in his saddle. After we had laid him down inside, he begged me to kill him, saying that if I was a friend of his I would put him out of his misery. I told him I was no friend of his kind who tried to murder me because I tried to do my duty; and I added that I did not shoot at my *friends* as he had been shot. Just then Mason entered the room again. O'Folliard at once changed his tone and cried, "Don't shoot any more, for God's sake. I am already kill- ed." Mason again told him to take his medicine. O'Folliard replied, "It's the best medicine I ever took." He also asked Mason to tell McKinney to write to his grandmother in Texas and inform her of his death. Once he exclaimed, "Oh, my God, is it possible that I must die?" I said to him just before he died, "Tom, your time is short." He answer- ed, "The sooner the better; I will be out of pain then." He blamed no one and told us who had been in the Kid's party with him. He died in about three quarters of an hour after he was shot.

Pickett, who was riding by O'Folliard's side, was un- hurt but he was nearly scared to death. He went howling over the prairie yelling bloody murder and was lost until the next night. He ran his horse to exhaustion and then took out on foot, reaching Wilcox's ranch about dark. He had run his horse fully twenty-five miles in a north-easterly direction before the animal gave out and then had to walk twelve or fifteen miles to the ranch. There he hid himself in a haystack and remained there crouching in fear and trembling until he saw his companions ride in from the hills.

The Capture of Billy the Kid

Tom Pickett, a member of the Kid's gang who was captured at Stinking Springs.

The Kid, Rudabaugh, Bowdre, and Wilson first went to Wilcox's ranch where Rudabaugh got another horse. Then they lost no time in going to the hills from which they watched the ranch and the surrounding country all the next day with their field glasses. At dark they rode back to the house, when Pickett showed himself. It must have been amusing to witness this fellow's sudden change from abject cowardice to excessive bravado as soon as he realized he was actually alive and unharmed and had friends within reach to whom he could look for protection. He swaggered about and blew his own horn somewhat in this strain: "Boys, I got that damn long-legged fellow that hollered 'halt.' I had my gun lying on my saddle in front of me and just as he yelled I poured it into him. Oh, I got him sure."

The gang now reduced to five remained at Wilcox's ranch that night, depressed and disheartened. After a long consultation they concluded to send some one to Fort Sumner the next morning to spy out the lay of the land. They took turns at standing guard throughout the night to prevent surprise, and the next morning sent Wilcox's partner, Brazil, to the plaza. They had been made suspicious of treachery on the part of Wilcox and Brazil when they were so effectually surprised at the old hospital building, but had been entirely reassured by them after returning to the ranch.

Brazil came to me at Fort Sumner on the morning of the 20th of December. He described the condition of the crestfallen band of outlaws and said they had sent him in to gather news and report to them. I told him to return, and, as a ruse, to tell them that I was at Sumner with only Mason and three Mexicans and that I was considerably scared up and wanted to get back to Roswell but feared to leave the plaza. Brazil remained in town until the next day; then, when he was ready to start, I told him that, if he found the gang still at the ranch when he arrived there, he should remain; but if they had left, or should leave after his arrival, he was to come and report to me. I had it un-

The Capture of Billy the Kid

derstood further between us that, if he did not come to me before two o'clock in the morning, I would start for the ranch, and if I did not meet him on the road, I would feel sure that the Kid's gang were still at the ranch. Brazil went home and almost immediately returned, reaching Sumner about 12 o'clock in the night.

There was snow on the ground, and it was so desperately cold that Brazil's beard was full of icicles. He reported that the Kid and his four companions had taken supper at Wilcox's, then mounted their horses and departed. My party and I all started for the ranch immediately. I took the precaution to send Brazil ahead to see whether the gang had returned, while with my posse I took a circuitous route by Lake Ranch, a mile or two off the road, thinking they might be there. We reached the ranch, surrounded the house, found it vacant, and rode on toward Wilcox's. About three miles from there we met Brazil, who reported that the outlaws had not returned and showed me their trail in the snow.

After following this trail a short distance, I was convinced that they had made for Stinking Springs, where there was an old deserted house, built by Alejandro Perea. When within a half mile of the house, we halted and held a consultation. I told my companions that I was confident we had them trapped, and cautioned them to preserve silence. We moved quietly in the direction of the house until we were only about four hundred yards distant; then we divided our party, leaving Juan Roibal in charge of the horses. Taking one-half of our force with me, I circled the house. I found a dry arroyo, and by taking advantage of its bed we were able to approach pretty close. Stewart, with the rest of the posse, found concealment on the other side within about two hundred yards of the building. We could see three horses tied to the porch rafters of the house, and knowing there were five in the gang and that they all mounted when they left Wilcox's, we concluded that they must have led two horses inside. There was no door to the house—just an opening where a door had once been. I had a messenger creep around to Stewart and propose that as the Kid's gang were surely there we stealthily enter the house, cover them with our guns, and hold them until daylight. Stewart did not view the suggestion favorably, although Lee Hall was decidedly in favor of it. So, shivering with cold, we awaited daylight or some movement on the part of the inmates of the house.

I had a perfect description of the Kid's dress, especially his hat. I had told all the posse that if the Kid made his appearance it was my intention to kill him, for then the rest would probably surrender. The Kid had sworn that he would never give himself up a prisoner, and would die

The Capture of Billy the Kid

Ash Upson, Garrett's close friend, assisted Pat with the writing of his book on Billy the Kid.

fighting even though there was a revolver at each ear, and I knew he would keep his word. I was in a position to command a view of the doorway, and I instructed my men that when I brought up my gun they should all raise theirs and fire. Before it was fully daylight, a man appeared at the entrance with a horse's nosebag in his hand, and I took him to be the Kid. His size and dress, especially the hat, corresponded exactly with the description I had been given of the Kid. So I gave a signal by bringing my gun to my shoulder; my men did likewise and seven bullets sped on their errand of death.

Our victim was Charlie Bowdre. He turned and reeled back into the house. In a moment Wilson called to me from the house and said that Bowdre was killed and wanted to come out. I told him to come out with his hands up. As he started, the Kid caught hold of his belt, drew his revolver around in front of him and said, "They have murdered you, Charlie, but you can get revenge. Kill some of the sons of b——s before you die." Bowdre came out with his pistol still hanging in front of him, but with his hands up. He walked unsteadily towards our group until he recognized me; then he came straight to me, motioning towards the house, and almost strangling with blood, said, "I wish—Iwish—Iwish—" then in a whisper, "I am dying!" I took hold of him, laid him gently on my blankets, and he died almost immediately.

As I watched in the increasing daylight every movement about the house, I shortly saw a movement of one of the ropes by which the horses were tied, and I surmised that the outlaws were attempting to lead one of the horses-inside. My first impulse was to shoot the rope in two, but it was shaking so that I was confident I would only miss. I did better than I expected, for just as the horse was fairly in the door opening, I shot him and he fell dead, partially barricading the outlet. To prevent another attempt of this kind, I shot in two the ropes which held the other horses and they promptly walked away. But the Kid and his companions still had two horses inside the house, one of them the Kid's favorite mare, celebrated for speed, bot-

tom, and beauty. I now opened a conversation with the besieged, the Kid acting as their spokesman. I asked him how
he was fixed in there.

"Pretty well," answered the Kid, "but we have no
wood to get breakfast with."

"Come out," said I, "and get some. Be a little socia-
ble."

"Can't do it, Pat," replied the Kid, "business is too
confining. No time to run around."

"Didn't you fellows forget a part of your program
yesterday?" said I. "You know you were to come in on us
at Fort Sumner from some other direction, give us a square
fight, set us afoot, and drive us down the Pecos."

Brazil had told me that, when he took the information to the Kid that I had only Mason and three Mexicans
with me at Sumner and was afraid to leave for home, the
Kid had proposed to come and "take me in." Bowdre,
however, had objected to the attempt, and the idea was
abandoned. My banter now caused the Kid to catch on to
the fact that they had been betrayed, and he became very
reticent in his subsequent remarks.

Those in our party were becoming very hungry, and,
getting together in one group, we arranged to go to Wilcox's ranch for breakfast. I went first, accompanied by
one-half of the other men. The distance was only about

three miles. When we reached there, Brazil asked me what news I brought. I told him that the news was bad; that we had killed the very man we didn't want to kill. When he learned it was Bowdre, he said, "I don't see why you should be sorry for having killed him. After you had that interview with him the other day, and was doing your best to get him out of his trouble, he said to me riding home, 'I wish you would get that son of a b—— out to meet me once more. I would just kill him and end all this trouble!' Now, how sorry are you?" I made arrangements with Wilcox to haul out to our camp some provisions together with wood and forage for our horses. I had no way to tell how long the outlaws might hold out, and I concluded I would make it as comfortable as possible for myself and the boys. The night previous Charlie Rudolph had frozen his feet slightly. When I and those who had gone with me returned, Stewart and the balance of the boys went to breakfast.

About three o'clock in the afternoon the gang turned loose the two horses from the inside. We picked them up as we had the other two. About four o'clock the wagon arrived from Wilcox's with the provisions and wood, and we built a rousing fire and went to cooking. The odor of roasting meat was too much for the famished lads who were without provisions. Craving stomachs overcame brave hearts. Rudabaugh stuck out from the window a handker-

The Capture of Billy the Kid

chief that had once been white and called to us that they wanted to surrender. I told them they could all come out with their hands up if they wanted to. Rudabaugh then came out to our camp and said they would all surrender if I would guarantee them protection from violence. This, of course, I did readily. Rudabaugh then returned to the house where he and the others held a short consultation. In a few minutes all of them—the Kid, Wilson, Pickett, and Rudabaugh—came out, were disarmed, given their supper, and started in our custody to Wilcox's. Brazil, Mason, and Rudolph I sent back from the ranch with a wagon after the body of Bowdre. They brought the corpse down to Wilcox's ranch, and, after a short stay, my party and I started for Fort Sumner, getting there before night. We turned Bowdre's body over to his wife, put irons on the prisoners, and by sundown Stewart, Mason, Jim East, "Poker Tom," and myself started for Las Vegas with our prisoners.

During the trip the Kid and Rudabaugh were cheerful and gay, Wilson somewhat dejected, and Pickett was badly frightened. The Kid said that if they had succeeded in leading the three horses, or two of them, or even one of them, into the house he and his crowd would have made a break and got away. He said also that he alone would have made a target out of himself until his mare could carry him out of the range of our guns or we had killed him—all of which might have been done had it not been for the dead horse barring his way. He said he knew his mare would not try to pass that body of a dead horse, and if she had tried to do so, she would have probably knocked the top of his head off against the lintel of the doorway. While at Fort Sumner the Kid had made Stewart a present of his mare, remarking in his usual joking way that he expected his business would be so confining for the next few months that he would hardly find time for horseback exercise.

We reached Gearhart's ranch with our prisoners about midnight, rested until eight in the morning, and reached Puerto de Luna at two o'clock in the afternoon on Christmas Day. My friend Grzelachowski gave us all a splendid dinner. My ubiquitous Don Quixote Arragan proffered to me again his invaluable services together with those of his original mob, which I respectfully declined. With a fresh team we got away from Puerto de Luna about four o'clock; but we had not travelled far before our wagon broke down and we were compelled to borrow one of Captain Clancy. We managed, however, to reach Hay's ranch in time for breakfast.

At two o'clock in the afternoon, December 26th, we reached Las Vegas and through a crowd of citizens made our way to the jail. Our objective point was the Santa Fe

The Capture of Billy the Kid

jail, as there were United States warrants against all our prisoners except Pickett. We intended to leave him at Las Vegas, but we proposed to go on with the other three to Santa Fe the next morning, although we expected, and so did Rudabaugh himself, that the authorities at Las Vegas would insist on holding him for the killing of the jailer. We had made a promise to Rudabaugh that we would take him to Santa Fe and we were determined to do it at all hazards. So Stewart went before an alcalde and made oath that we were holding this prisoner on a United States warrant; this affidavit and our warrant, we believed, would enable us to hold Rudabaugh as our prisoner and take him to Santa Fe.

On the morning of December 27th, I had fresh irons placed on the Kid, Rudabaugh, and Wilson. As Michael Cosgrove, the mail contractor carrying the mail from Fort Sumner to Roswell, was well acquainted in Santa Fe, I induced him to accompany me there with the prisoners, and I therefore released two of my guards, starting with only Cosgrove, Stewart, and Mason. After breakfast we went to the jail for our prisoners. They turned over the Kid and Wilson to us and we handcuffed them together. Then we demanded Rudabaugh, but they refused to give him up, saying that he had escaped from that jail and that he was wanted for a murder committed in Las Vegas. I argued with them that my right to the prisoner outranked theirs inasmuch as I was a deputy United States marshal and had arrested Rudabaugh for an offense against the laws of the United States and was not supposed to be cognizant of any other offense or arrest. I insisted that I was responsible for him as my prisoner and pressed in no uncertain terms my intention to have him. Stewart drew his affidavit on them and they at last turned Rudabaugh over to us.

We had been on the train with our three prisoners but a few minutes when we noticed that a good many Mexicans scattered through the crowd were armed with rifles and revolvers and seemed considerably excited. Stewart and I concluded that their object was to take Rudabaugh off the train. I asked Stewart whether we should make a fight for it if such an attempt was made. He said we would, of course, do so; and I replied, "Let's make a good one." We felt sure that they intended to mob Rudabaugh then and there, and for that further reason were unwilling to give him up. He acknowledged that he was afraid of them, and we were moreover under pledge to protect him and take him to Santa Fe. Stewart guarded one door of the car and I the other. These armed ruffians crowded about the car, but none of them made a formal demand for Rudabaugh or stated their business. Deputy Sheriff Romero, brother of the sheriff, who had so distinguished himself when I brought Webb to him at Hay's ranch, headed a mob

The Capture of Billy the Kid

In May of 1979, the site of the rock house at Stinking Springs was visited by Jarvis Garrett, the youngest son of Pat Garrett.

of five, who approached the car platform where I was standing, and flourished their revolvers. One of them said, "Let's go right in and take him out of there," and with that they began to push the deputy up the car steps, while the others crowded after him. I merely requested them in my mildest tones to get down, and they slid to the ground like a covey of hard-back turtles off the banks of the Pecos. They did not seem so much frightened as modest and bashful.

Rudabaugh was of course excited; the Kid and Wilson seemed unconcerned. I told all three not to be uneasy, for

Pat Garrett

Jarvis Garrett stands near the foundation of the rock house at Stinking Springs.

we intended to make a fight if the mob tried to enter the car; and I added that, if the fight came off, I would arm them and let them take a hand. The Kid's eyes glistened as he said, "All right, Pat. All I want is a six-shooter." Then, as he looked out at the crowd, he remarked, "There is no danger though. Those fellows won't fight." He was correct in his observation, for those in the mob were evidently weakening and all they wanted was for some one to coax them to desist so it would not look like a square back-down. Some influential Mexicans began to reason with them and they quickly subsided. We were detained by

The Capture of Billy the Kid

them about three-quarters of an hour. I understood afterwards that they had covered the engineer with their guns and threatened him if he moved the train. One of the railroad officials had thereupon warned them of danger from the law for detaining the United States mail. Finally Mollay, a deputy United States marshal who had had some railroad experience, mounted the cab and pulled the train out.

I had telegraphed to Charles Conklin, deputy United States marshal at Santa Fe, and when the train arrived, I found him at the depot waiting for us. I turned the prisoners over to him on the 27th of December, and he placed them in the Santa Fe jail.

One of the last photographs of Patrick Floyd Garrett that was probably taken in about 1906.

The Capture of Billy the Kid

The only known photograph taken of Sheriff Pat Garrett in 1881, the year in which he killed Billy the Kid..

118

NEWSPAPER REPORTS

The capture of Billy the Kid was front page news in New Mexico. The newly elected sheriff, Pat F. Garrett, had come onto the scene in a blaze of glory, having captured the Kid even before he had been sworn into office. The Kid, Tom Pickett, Billy Wilson, and Dave Rudabaugh were in jail and two of the Kid's pals, O'Folliard and Bowdre, were buried at Fort Sumner.

Since the Kid was jailed temporarily at Las Vegas, reporters from the GAZETTE and the DAILY OPTIC conducted the first interviews with the new sheriff and the outlaws. These two versions are included in this book to provide another interpretation of the event.

These two versions and previous ones in this volume, have agreed on many points, and have disagreed on others. Undoubtedly, an absolutely accurate version may never be determined.

119

The Capture of Billy the Kid

Las Vegas Gazette, December 27, 1880.

"THE KID"

The greatest excitement prevailed yesterday afternoon when the news was noised abroad that Pat Garrett and Frank Stewart had arrived in town bringing with them Billy "the Kid," the notorious outlaw and three of his gang. People stood on the muddy street corners and in hotel offices and saloons talking of the great event. The excitement and interest can scarcely be imagined for four days our people have been highly expectant to learn news from the parties in search of the desparados who have been depredating the Pecos and White Oaks country and when it was found that the nucleus of the band was captured they were at first dazed by the astonishing news of the success of the brave, determined men. Astonishment gave way to joy when the real truth was known. Groups of people flocked to the jail and hung around the corners straining their necks to catch a glimpse of Sheriff Garrett, Frank Stewart and the brave fellows who had brought in the outlaws. But they went quietly from the jail to the corral and from there to the National House where the half-starved, tired men sought to escape the scrutinizing gaze of the scores of hero worshippers.

120

Newspapers

A little after 4 o'clock yesterday afternoon a two-mule wagon hauling four or five men besides the driver, with three men on horseback came at a good gait up the old Santa Fe trail. They kept on past the plaza and drew up at the jail. The few who were on the streets followed the little cavalcade, but their curiosity was only slightly satisfied, for without any ceremony, the crowd was quickly within the jail.

The announcement was made that the party comprised Billy "the Kid," captain of the gang that has been making its headquarters at Las Portales; Dave Rudabaugh, his desperate lieutenant who killed Lopez the jailer in this city the first of last April; Billy Wilson, the slick young fellow who has been passing counterfeit money, and Tom Pickett, the ex-policeman of Vegas who was reported to have been killed in Sumner one week ago. News of their arrival ran like wildfire about town and everyone was on the que vive for particulars of the capture.

A representative of the GAZETTE sought out Sheriff Garrett and had a short talk with him, but this modest man who has little to say, but is always ready for action, turned him over to Mr. M.S. Bazil, whom he said knew all the particulars.

The Capture of Billy the Kid

Accompanying Mr. Bazil to the residence of Mr. T.W. Garrard the GAZETTE man was told the story of this last successful campaign.

After the affair at Jim Greathouse's ranch, the details of which were published in the GAZETTE a few days ago, "the Kid" and his remaining followers thought it about time to leave the country. They went to the ranch of T.Z. Yerby and hung around there and the ranch of Mr. Bazil for some days, making frequent visits to Ft. Sumner.

While they were rusticating about fifteen or twenty miles from here a Mexican living on Buffalo Arroyo, named Lojino Anala, came into Sumner, while a few of Garrett's party were there. It was thought by some that it would not be wise to allow him to go out again as it was intended to keep all news of the whereabouts of the party in search of the outlaws from them. A few suggested that he be detained till after the party set out, but he was finally permitted to go on his way. On the road home near Alamo Gordo Lojilo met Bob Campbell, who was formerly employed by Mr. Bazil, and told him that Garrett and five men were already at Sumner and that more men were expected there. Campbell straightway rode off to find "the Kid" and gang, and meeting them on the road, they fell back and secreted themselves. Two or three days later, Garrett's party left Sumner and Bob Campbell learning of this went to Bazil's ranch and hired a Mexican boy, about 16 years old, to take a note to Yerby's ranch telling the gang that the coast was all clear. The crowd were then making arrangements to leave the country but were anxious to get supplies and so they would venture into Sumner. Charley Bowder, who was recently so clamorous for a vindication from the charge of being a desperado, that was made against him in the GAZETTE, had been enticed by "the Kid" to join him. It is thought by many that the latter, who has a faculty for making friends with everybody, attracted Charley to him. They had both been concerned in the Lincoln county war and Charley knowing there was a U. S. Warrant out for his arrest for a murder committed in Lincoln made arrangements to skip the country with them. On the 19th, Tom O'Foliard and Tom Pickett, "the Kid" and Rudabaugh, and Charley Bowdre and Billy Wilson, riding two and two, came into Sumner just about dark. Garrett and his men had returned and when the six come around the northeast corner of the hospital building, Garrett, who was in advance, ordered them to halt. O'Foliard and Pickett were in front and the former reached for his six-shooter but was not quick enough for Garrett who fired first, bringing down O'Foliard. The other five put spurs to their horses and rode away under cover of a heavy fire from the attacking party. It was

123

The Capture of Billy the Kid

thought that Pickett was shot, as pools of blood were discovered, but this was a mistake, only O'Foliard being shot, besides one horse. The night was so foggy that the others got away safely. They made Bazil's, and Rudabaugh's horse was found to be badly shot through the entrails, and it is a wonder it did not die on the way. Rudabaugh and one of the others doubled up and they made off as fast as they could.

Tom O'Foliard lived only two hours after being shot.

Word was brought to Garrett at Sumner that the crowd were hanging around Bazil's and Yerby's ranch and Wednesday night sixteen men under command of Garrett set out for Bazil's ten miles east of Sumner. They arrived there about midnight and learned that "the Kid", Rudabaugh, Wilson, Pickett and Bowdre had been there during the afternoon but had ridden away again. About three or four inches of snow was on the ground, and the moon being out it was easy to follow their trail. Following it up at about 3 o'clock they came to an old deserted house at Stinking Springs four miles away near the junction of the Canunditas and Alamosa where they found the men. They divided into several parties and keeping guard on the house lay down to wait till daybreak.

The house is built of stone with a door and window

on one side. It is situated about six or seven steps from the arroyo, on the top of a hill.

Just at daybreak Charlie Bowdre came to the door and stepped out. He had a hat like what "the Kid" had repeatedly been wearing, and he was mistaken for him. "The Kid" had repeatedly given out that he would never surrender, even though a six-shooter were placed to his head, that it wasn't thought worth while to give him a chance to surrender. Someone fired and Bowdre staggered and then bracing himself up for a moment against the door-post stepped into the house. He told his companions that he was badly wounded and could not assist them any and wanted to go out, and calling to the men outside the situation was explained. Bowdre stepped out again and started forward to give himself up when he reeled a little and said: "I wish–," and while making an effort to express his desire, he fell dead close by where one of the beseigers was lying concealed.

Quiet prevailed all day, the besiegers determined to stay until they carried away the outlaws dead or alive. The outlaws had two horses in the house with them and about 4 o'clock were discovered trying to drag in a third. They had his head and shoulders just inside the door when Garrett brought it down and it fell on the door step blocking up the entrance to the house. Two other horses

The Capture of Billy the Kid

were tied outside the house and the besiegers amused themselves by shooting at their halters and succeeded in cutting them loose. The intention of the gang was to get the third horse inside the house and then all four were to make a break on horseback. But they were forced to give up this plan as the body of the dead horse was a blockade against them. A consultation was held and Rudabaugh, Wilson and Pickett voted to surrender much to the disgust of "the Kid" who kicked and kicked, but to no avail. He branded the others as cowards but was unable to dissuade them from their project to surrender.

Finally, some of the attacking party saw a rag being twirled about the end of a stick stuck through the door which was mistrusted to be a flag of truce. Remembering the fate of poor Carlyle at Greathouse's, Garrett said that two could play at that game and let the crowd inside a- muse themselves by waving the stick. He called out to them to know what they wanted when Rudabaugh an- nounced that they wanted to surrender. They had not counted on such an easy capture and felt that the despera- does were playing some game. But in response to the call "come out then," Rudabaugh advanced and talked with Garrett and some of the men.

He offered to surrender conditionally, provided the party would take them to Santa Fe, and everything being

126

arranged, he returned to the house again. A short time only elapsed before they all filed out and gave themselves up.

They were mounted with some of their captors and the party moved on to Bazil's house, sending back a team for the guns and outfit of the gang which they had left in the house.

The two horses which had been stabled in the house belonged to "the Kid" and Billy Wilson and the former made a present of his to Frank Stewart. "The Kid's" animal is a beautiful bay mare, which he has always trusted in to take him out of a tight place, and has shared his love in common with his guns. Stewart now has the pleasure of owning the fleetest horse in the territory.

Among the attacking party was Lojilo, the Mexican, who had given information of Garrett's presence in Sumner, and whom the latter captured and forced to take part in the search for the outlaws.

The party spent the night at Bazil's where Rudabaugh and "the Kid" were chained together. The body of Bowdre was taken to the house and it was found that he had been shot through the right breast the ball coming out in the neck.

Just after sunrise Friday morning the party set out for Sumner, with the body of Bowdre, and leaving that

127

The Capture of Billy the Kid

came on towards Vegas with a guard of nine men keeping watch over the prisoners, who were placed in Mr. Bazil's wagon. They reached Gerhardt's ranch about 10 o'clock that night and remained till night setting out the next morning again. Arriving at Puerta de Luna Saturday night about sundown they stopped long enough to change horses and chain Pickett and Wilson together, who until that time had not been bound. Here four of the guards left them and the rest traveled all night, and on the way the lock fastening the chain binding Wilson and Pickett was broken, but a sharp lookout was kept on them. They took breakfast at Mr. Hayes's yesterday morning about 10 o'clock and then came right through, arriving at the jail late in the afternoon as has been stated.

Besides Pat Garrett and Frank Stewart, in the party who brought the gang into Vegas, there were J.N. East and F.W. Emory of the Panhandle and Barney Mason.

Garrett and some of his men guarded the prisoners carefully at the jail, it being their intention to take "the Kid" and Billy Wilson to Santa Fe today, as they are wanted for counterfeiting as well as for other crimes. Rudabaugh and Pickett will be kept in our jail.

The party was intending to slip out of the country the morning that they were attacked so that the pursuing party were none too soon in coming up with them.

128

A newly discovered photograph that is believed to be that of Billy the Kid. (Copyrighted by Creative Publishing Co.)

129

The Capture of Billy the Kid

Billy "the Kid" explains that they thought that the besiegers were stronger than what they really were, and that it would have been certain death to have attempted to get away. "Life is sweet if it is behind prison bars" exclaimed Billy. But the "Kid" will have enough of it to sour him, if we mistake not.

The campaign has been a credit to the brave fellows who have participated in it, and we congratulate Sheriff Garrett and all his men for the successful issue of their round-up.

Las Vegas Daily Optic, December 27, 1880.

A BIG HAUL!

Billy Kid, Dave Rudabaugh, Billy Wilson and Tom Pickett in the clutches of the law.

. . . . . .

A Notorious Gang of Outlaws Broken up, and the Country Breathes Easier.

. . . .

Our readers are familiar with the depredations committed in the lower country by a gang of daring desperadoes, under the leadership of Billy Kid, and the repeated and unsuccessful attempts to capture them. They have roamed over the country at will, placing no value upon human life, and appropriating the property of ranchmen and travellers without stint. Posses of men have been in hot pursuit of them for weeks, but they suceeded in eluding their pursuers every time. However, the right boys started out, well mounted and heavily armed, and were successful in bagging their game.

Yesterday afternoon
the town was thrown into a fever of excitement by an announcement that the "Kid" and other members of his gang of outlaws had been captured, and were nearing the city. The rumor was soon verified by the appearance in town of a squad of men led by Pat Garrett, deputy sheriff of Lincoln county, and Frank Stewart, of the Panhandle country, having in custody the Kid, Dave Rudabaugh, Billy Wilson and Tom Pickett. They were taken at once to the jail against any attempt to take the prisoners out and hang them. Feeling was particularly strong against Rudabaugh, who was an accessory to the murder of the Mexican jailor in an attempt to release Webb some months ago.

The Pursuit of the Gang
It will be remembered that Frank Stewart, with a

131

The Capture of Billy the Kid

party of picked men, left Las Vegas on December 14th, to join Pat Garrett and his squad, who were in waiting at Fort Sumner. The boys made a quick trip of it, arriving at the designated place of meeting on the night of the 17th instant. Nothing unusual transpired until the following night, when Kid's party approached the place, for the purpose of cleaning out Garrett's squad, not knowing that reinforcements had come. Precaution had been taken to place a guard on the outside of the house, and upon hearing

The Clatter of Horses' Hoofs

in the distance, he warned his companions of the danger and they at once prepared to give the outlaws a warm reception. The night was very dark and foggy and even moving objects could be seen only at a very short distance. The first rider who came in range of the trusty Winchesters was Tom O'Foliard who fell dead from his horse under the unerring aim of a half-dozen frontiersmen. Tom Pickett was following immediately behind, but, after the first volley, he turned his horse and

Fled For His Life.

Pursuit was out of the question, owing to the intense darkness that prevailed and the additional fact that a heavy storm had set in. Dave Rudabaugh's horse was shot but

132

succeeded in carrying his rider a distance of twelve miles before dropping dead. The

Party Of Plucky Pursuers
now laid over two days starting forward on the evening of the third day, the 23rd. Promptly at the hour of twelve, they mounted their horses and rode twelve miles, to Wilcox's ranch. Here it was obtained that Kid and his followers had taken supper there the night before and were at their rendezvous, a vacant stone house, about three miles farther on. After a few moments' halt the brave pursuers, for such they proved themselves to be, put spurs to their horses and rode quietly to the house designated as the hiding place of Kid's men. Upon approaching the premises, at 2 o'clock in the morning, three horses were seen hitched to the front door ready to be mounted.

At A Second's Notice.
Garrett and Stewart at once surrounded the house, giving their men instructions to lay flat in the snow and await further developments.

Just At Daybreak
on the morning of the 24th a man supposed to be the Kid, but afterwards proving to be Charles Bowdre, appeared at

The Capture of Billy the Kid

the door. His body was pierced by two balls almost in an instant. The signal for shooting was given immediately upon the appearance of Bowdre, as Kid, who is a sure shot, had often boasted that he would never be taken alive. The only way to capture him was to shoot him down at sight. The killing of Bowdre alarmed those upon the inside of the house and they endeavored to ascertain what party was in pursuit of them; however, their calling elicited no response. Two of the three horses standing at the door were

Shot Down In Their Tracks,

and the third one was shot in the doorway while Kid was in the act of getting the animal upon the inside out of the reach of the deadly bullets. The carcass of the dead horse across the threshold prevented the Kid from leaping upon his horse, which was in the room with him, and attempting to escape. About 4 o'clock in the afternoon, the surrounded party

Displayed a Flag

and Rudabaugh walked out boldly and said that they were willing to surrender, provided they were guaranteed protection. This was promised them and, in turn, "Kid", Billy Wilson and Tom Pickett joined Rudabaugh upon the outside and gave themselves up to their captors, who put their

134

prisoners on horses, doubling up as occasion required, and rode back to Wilcox's ranch, from which place a wagon was sent back after the young arsenal left at the robbers' rendezvous. The captors and their prisoners remained at the ranch all night, starting for Las Vegas on Christmas morning and arriving here before supper last night--very rapid riding.

The party of men
Who Risked Their Lives
in the attempt to rid the country of this bloodthirsty gang of robbers and murderers are deserving of unbounded praise and should be rewarded handsomely for their services. They will undoubtedly obtain the reward of $500 offered by the Governor for the capture of Kid, and it remains for interested citizens to raise a purse of money and present it to these sixteen men, as they have paid out money and endured hardships in the endeavor to hunt down and bring to justice one of the most desperate gangs of outlaws that ever terrorized the southwest.

THE PRISONERS

Kid is about 24 years of age, and has a bold yet pleasant cast of countenance. When interviewed between the bars at the jail this morning, he was in a talkative mood, but said that anything he might say would not be believed by the people. He laughed heartily when informed that the papers of the Territory had built him up a reputation second only to that of Victorio. Kid claims never to have had a large number of men with him, and that the few who were with him when captured were employed on a ranch. This is his statement and is given for what it is worth.

DAVE RUDABAUGH

looks and dresses about the same as when in Las Vegas, apparently not having made any raids upon clothing stores. His face is weather-beaten from long exposure. This is the only noticeable difference. Rudabaugh inquired somewhat anxiously in regard to the feeling in the community and was told that it was very strong against him. He remarked that the papers had all published exaggerated reports of the depredations of Kid's party in the lower country. It was not half so bad as has been reported.

TOM PICKETT.

Tom, who was once a policeman in West Las Vegas, greeted everybody with a hearty grip of the hand and seemed reasonably anxious to undergo an examination. Pickett is well connected, but has led a wild career. His father lives in Decatur, Wise county, Texas, and has served as a member

of the Legislature. All the home property was once mort-
gaged to keep Pickett out of prison, but he unfeelingly
skipped the country, betraying the confidence of his own
mother.

BILLY WILSON,

the other occupant of the cell, reclined leisurely on some
blankets in the corner of the apartment and his medita-
tions were not disturbed by our Faber pusher.

GREATHOUSE IMPLICATED.

There remains no doubt of the fact that James
Greathouse was a member of Kid's marauding party. Letters written by him to the talented rascal were intercepted
in the mails. At one time he furnished horses for Kid and
his followers to escape from his ranch and, while in Las
Vegas, wrote to Kid warning him to leave the country or
he would be captured. While in town he dispatched a
courier to Bell's ranch for a horse, which he undoubtedly
obtained and rode home on.

OFF FOR SANTA FE.

Billy Kid, Billy Wilson and Dave Rudabaugh, under
the escort of Pat Garrett, Frank Stewart, Mr. Cosgrove and
one or two others, were taken to Santa Fe this afternoon.

137

The Capture of Billy the Kid

As the train was ready to leave the depot, an unsuccessful attempt was made by Sheriff Romero to secure Ruda-baugh and return him to the county jail. The engineer of the outgoing train was covered by guns, and ordered not to move his engine. If the sheriff had been as plucky as some of the citizens who urged him forward, the matter would have been settled without any excitement whatever. The prisoner, Rudabaugh, the only one wanted, was virtually in the hands of the United States authorities, having been arrested by deputy United States marshals, and they were in duty bound to deliver him to the authorities in Santa Fe. The sheriff and a few picked, trusty men, might have gone over to Santa Fe with the party, and, after Rudabough's delivery, brought him back to Las Vegas, where he is badly wanted, not only by the Mexicans, but by all Americans who desire to see the law vindicated.

Las Vegas Gazette, December 28, 1880.

THE KID

Interview With Billy Bonney The Best Known Man in
New Mexico.

With its accustomed enterprise the GAZETTE was

the first paper to give the story of the capture of Billy Bonney, who has risen to notoriety under the sobriquet of "the Kid," Billy Wilson, Dave Rudabaugh, and Tom Pickett. Just at this time everything of interest about the men is especially interesting and after damning the party in general and "the Kid" in particular, through the columns of this paper we considered it the correct thing to give them a show.

Through the kindness of Sheriff Romero, a representative of the GAZETTE was admitted to the jail yesterday morning.

Mike Cosgrove, the obliging mail contractor, who has often met the boys while on business down the Pecos, had just gone in with four large bundles. The doors at the entrance stood open and a large crowd strained their necks to get a glimpse of the prisoners, who stood in the passageway like children waiting for a Christmas tree distribution. One by one the bundles were unpacked disclosing a good suit of clothes for each man. Mr. Cosgrove remarked that he wanted "to see the boys go away in style."

"Billy, the Kid" and Billy Wilson who were shackled together stood patiently up while a blacksmith took off

139

The Capture of Billy the Kid

their shackles and bracelets to allow them an opportunity to make a change of clothing. Both prisoners watched the operation which was to set them free for a short while, but Wilson scarcely raised his eyes and spoke but once or twice to his compadre. Bonney, on the other hand, was light and chipper and was very communicative, laughing, joking and chatting with the bystanders.

"You appear to take it easy" the reporter said.

"Yes! What's the use of looking on the gloomy side of everything. The laugh's on me this time," he said. Then looking about the placita, he asked "is the jail at Santa Fe any better than this?"

This seemed to trouble him considerably, for, as he explained "this is a terrible place to put a fellow in." He put the same question to every one who came near him and when he learned that there was nothing better in store for him, he shrugged his shoulders and said something about putting up with what he had to.

He was the attraction of the show, and as he stood there, lightly kicking the toes of his boots on the stone pavement to keep his feet warm, one would scarcely mistrust that he was the hero of the "Forty Thieves" romance which this paper has been running in serial form for six weeks or more.

"There was a big crowd gazing at me wasn't there," he exclaimed, and then smilingly continued "Well, perhaps some of them will think of me half man now; everyone seems to think I was some kind of an animal."

He did look human, indeed, but there was nothing very mannish about him in appearance, for he looked and acted a mere boy. He is about five feet eight or nine inches tall, slightly built and lithe, weighing about 140; a frank open countenance, looking like a school boy, with the traditional silky fuzz on his upper lip; clear blue eyes, with a rougish snap about them; light hair and complexion. He is, in all, quite a handsome looking fellow, the only imperfection being two prominent front teeth slightly protruding like squirrel's teeth, and he has agreeable and winning ways.

A cloud came over his face when he made some allusions to his being made the hero of fabulous yarns, and something like indignation was expressed when he said that our Extra misrepresented him in saying that he called his associates cowards. "I never said any such a thing," he pouted. "I know they ain't cowards."

Billy Wilson was glum and sober, but from underneath his broad-brimmed hat, we saw a face that had a by no means bad look. He is a light complexioned, light haired, bluish-gray eyes, is a little stouter than Bonney, and far quieter. He appeared ashamed and not in very good spirits.

A final stroke of the hammer sent the last rivet on the bracelets, and they clanked on the pavement as they fell.

Bonney straightened up and then rubbing his wrists, where the sharp edged irons had chafed him, said:

"I don't suppose you fellows would believe it but this is the first time I ever had bracelets on. But many another better fellow has had them on too."

With Wilson he walked towards the little hole in the wall to the place, which is no "sell" on a place of confinement. Just before entering he turned and looked back and exclaimed: "They say, 'a fool for luck and a poor man for children'—Garrett takes them all in."

We saw him again at the depot when the crowd presented a really warlike appearance. Standing by the car,

142

An early drawing of Billy the Kid that appeared in Fable's THE TRUE LIFE OF BILLY THE KID.

out of one of the windows of which he was leaning, he talked freely with us of the whole affair.

"I don't blame you for writing of me as you have. You had to believe others stories; but then I don't know as any one would believe anything good of me anyway." he said. "I wasn't the leader of any gang—I was for Billy all the time. About that Portales business, I owned the rancho with Charlie Bowdre. I took it up and was holding it because I wanted to keep it for a station. But, I found that there were certain men who wouldn't let me live in the country and so I was going to leave. We had all our grub in the house when they took us in, and we were going to a place about six miles away in the morning to cook it and then 'light' out. I haven't stolen any stock. I made my liv-

The Capture of Billy the Kid

ing by gambling but that was the only way I could live. They wouldn't let me settle down; if they had I wouldn't be here today." and he held up his right arm on which was the bracelet. "Chisum got me into all this trouble and then wouldn't help me out. I went up to Lincoln to stand my trial on the warrant that was out for me, but the territory took a change of venue to Dona Ana, and I knew that I had no show, and so I skinned out. When I went up to White Oaks the last time, I went there to consult with a lawyer, who had sent for me to come up. But I knew I couldn't stay there either."

The conversation then drifted to the question of the final round-up of the party. Billy's story is the same as that given in our Extra, issued at midnight on Sunday.

"If it hadn't been for the dead horse in the doorway I wouldn't be here. I would have ridden out on my bay mare and taken my chances of escaping" said he. "But I couldn't ride out over that, for she would have jumped back, and I would have got it in the head. We could have staid in the house but there wouldn't have been anything gained by that for they would have starved us out. I thought it was better to come out and get a good square meal—don't you?"

144

*Jim East, as he
appeared in his
later years.*

The prospects of a fight exhilarated him, and he bitterly bemeaned being chained. "If I only had my Winchester, I'd lick the whole crowd" was his confident comment on the strength of the attacking party. He sighed and sighed again for a chance to take a hand in the fight and the burden of his desire was to be set free to fight on the side of his captors as soon as he should smell powder.

As the train rolled out, he lifted his hat and invited us to call and see him in Santa Fe, calling out adios.

145

The Capture of Billy the Kid

Las Vegas Daily Optic, December 31, 1880.

Acting Governor Ritch, in the absence of Governor Wallace, did not feel authorized to pay the reward of five hundred dollars offered by the Territory for the apprehension of Billy Kid; however, the citizens of Santa Fe raised that amount and gave it to Garrett and Stewart, accepting their order for the money.

Las Vegas Morning Gazette, Tuesday, January 4, 1881.

A BRAG-MARE

Every one who has heard of Billy "the Kid" has heard of his beautiful bay mare, about whose speed some remarkable stories are told. Billy kept the beautiful mare very carefully and always reserves her for an emergency, fully appreciating her good qualities, and knowing full well that no other animal could run her down. There is no doubt in the minds of those who are most competent to judge but what she is the best animal in New Mexico. She was purchased from Texas stockmen a few years ago and whenever put to the test has demonstrated the fact that she was a remarkable piece of horseflesh. When Billy was besieged in the old stone house at Stinking Springs by the

Stewart Garrett party, he intended to make a break for liberty on her back Mazoppa-like, and expected that her fleetness would carry him out of harm's reach and from the bullets of the "dead shots" who were lying in wait for him. But the doorway being blockaded by the dead body of a horse he was hemmed in. When he was finally rounded-up, he presented the mare to Frank Stewart, knowing that he would appreciate her as he certainly did, and he afterwards rode her in triumph to Vegas. Those who have seen her have grown enthusiastic and it will be gratifying to

our horsemen to know that the mare will remain in our neighborhood. W. Scott Moore, proprietor of The Adobe at the Hot Springs, made Frank Stewart a New Year's present of an elegant revolver valued at $60 one of many gifts our citizens have presented the brave Stewart as a testimonial of their appreciation of his good work in the campaign against "the Kid's" band. Not to be outdone, Stewart in turn presented Mrs. Moore with "the Kid's" mare, and she now has the satisfaction of owning one of the best, if not the best animal in the territory.

* * * * * *

The Capture of Billy the Kid

BIBLIOGRAPHY

BOOKS

Garrett, Pat F. *The Authentic Life of Billy the Kid, the Noted Desperado of the Southwest.* Santa Fe: New Mexico Printing and Publishing Company, 1882.

Siringo, Charles A. *History of "Billy the Kid."* [Santa Fe, N. M.: Privately printed for the author, 1920.]

UNPUBLISHED MANUSCRIPTS

Bousman, Louis, Transcript of an interview with Bousman, Unpublished, written in 1934.

Foor, Charles W., Hand-drawn map of Old Fort Sumner, New Mexico, Drawn in 1927.

Polk, Cal, Unfinished biography, Unpublished, written in 1896.

NEWSPAPERS
Las Vegas, New Mexico, *Gazette*

Las Vegas, New Mexico, *Daily Optic*

149

The Capture of Billy the Kid

THE
EARLY WEST

PHOTOGRAPH CREDITS

We are appreciative of cooperation of the following agencies for permission to use photographs from their archives:

University of Arizona Library, Special Collections: Pages 36, 37, 38, 60, 106.

Panhandle Plains Museum: Pages 12, 41

Earle Collection: Pages 17, 44, 54, 55, 63, 65, 67, 68, 85, 90, 100, 114, 115, 118, 129

INDEX

Index

𝔗𝔥𝔢 𝔗𝔢𝔯𝔯𝔦𝔱𝔬𝔯𝔶 𝔬𝔣 𝔑𝔢𝔴 𝔍

To the Sheriff of _____ *Lincc*

You are hereby c

_____ *William Wilso*

keep so that you have his body before the

_____ *Lincoln* _____ at the

Court House in said County, on the _____ /

D. 188*2*, then and there to answer un

and this do under penalty of the law.

WITNESS *The H(*

the Sup

and Ju(

and the

of _____

156

ounty, Greeting :

led *To arrest and take the body of*

..and him safely

Court within and for the County of

hereof to be begun and held at the

onday of *July* *A.*

Redictminn *for*

y

EN BRISTOL, Associate Justice of

t of the Territory of New Mexico,

hird Judicial District Court thereof,

id Court this *26ᵗ* *day*

uber *A. D. 188/ .*

eR Bowman

Clerk.

157

532

Burglary

vs Murder

Wm Bonney alias Kid
alias William Antrim

Copy of Judgment

I certify that I recd the
prisoner named William
Bonney alias Kid alias
William Antrim into my
custody on the 21st day of
April A.D. 1881
and I further certify that
on April 28th the said Wm
Bonney alias Kid alias
William Antrim made
his escape by killing his
guard J.W. Bell and
Robt Ollinger in Lincoln
Lincoln Co. N.M.

Boarding children & four
weeks 6 days $40.00
Groceries & transport-
ing from Ft. _____ 69.00
50
returning April $109.50